THE HIGHWAY CODE

for Northern Ireland

AA Publishing

Produced by AA Publishing.
© AA Media Limited 2009

Pages 11–136 reproduced from *The Official Highway Code for Northern Ireland*. Department of the Environment.
© Crown Copyright 2008
Reproduced under the terms of the Click-Use Licence.

Published by AA Publishing (a trading name of AA Media Limited, whose registered office is Fanum House; Basing View, Basingstoke, Hampshire RG21 4EA; registered number 06112600).

ISBN 978-0-7495-6503-9

A04234

Visit the AA at theAA.com/shop

The contents of this book are believed correct at the time of printing. Nevertheless, the publishers cannot be held responsible for any errors or omissions or for changes in the details given in this book or for the consequences of any reliance on the information provided by the same. This does not affect your statutory rights.

Printed by Printer Trento, Italy

For more information about *The Highway Code for Northern Ireland* visit www.nidirect.gov.uk

Contents

Taking your Tests   **4**

The Highway Code   **11**

Introduction   **12**
Rules for pedestrians   13
Rules for powered wheelchairs
    and powered scooters   21
Rules about animals   23
Rules for cyclists   26
Rules for motorcyclists   31
Rules for drivers and motorcyclists   33
General rules, techniques and advice
    for all drivers and riders   38
Using the road   53
Road users requiring extra care   67
Driving in adverse weather conditions   72
Waiting and parking   75
Motorways   79
Breakdowns and incidents   83
Roadworks   87
Level crossings   88
Tramways   90
Light signals controlling traffic   92
Signals to other road users   93
Signals by authorised persons   94
Traffic signs   96
Road markings   104
Vehicle markings   107

Annexes
1. You and your bicycle   108
2. Motorcycle licence requirements   108
3. Motor vehicle documentation, learner
    and restricted driver requirements   110
4. The road user and the law   113
5. Penalties   115
6. Vehicle maintenance, safety
    and security   118
7. First aid on the road   121
8. Safety code for new drivers   122

Other information   **124**
Appendix   **126**
Index   **130**

Taking your Tests

Studying and getting to know the Highway Code section of this book is just one of the things you must do in order to help you pass your driving test. Before you apply for a full driving licence you must pass two tests – the Theory Test, including Hazard Perception, and the Practical Test. The Theory Test was introduced in 1996 to check that drivers know more than just how to operate a car, and the Hazard Perception element was introduced in 2001 to test learner drivers on their hazard awareness skills. This section explains the format of both parts of the driving test. It is followed by the Northern Ireland edition of the Highway Code on pages 11–129.

You are strongly recommended to prepare for the Theory Test and Hazard Perception at the same time as you develop your skills behind the wheel during practical instruction. Obviously, there are many similarities between the two tests and you need the experience of meeting real hazards in order to pass the Hazard Perception element of the Theory Test.

It is all about making you a safer driver on today's busy roads. By preparing for both tests at the same time, you will reinforce your knowledge and understanding of all aspects of driving and you will improve your chances of passing both tests first time.

The Practical Test also includes Vehicle Safety questions that test the driver's ability to carry out basic procedures to ensure that the vehicle is safe to drive. Checks include the tyre tread and oil level.

THE THEORY TEST

Once you have a provisional licence you may take the Theory Test at any time, but you must pass both elements (the Theory Test and the Hazard Perception test) before you can apply to take a Practical Test.

The paperwork

When reporting for your Theory Test you must bring your appointment letter and both parts of your valid signed Northern Ireland or GB driving licence. If your licence does not show your photograph, you must also bring with you a form of photographic identification, such as a current signed passport. A card such as a cheque guarantee or credit card, an employer's identity card, trade union card, but only if it is signed and has a photograph. For the full list of acceptable photographic ID, see the Driver & Vehicle Agency website, www.dvani.gov.uk

What to expect in the Theory Test

You will have 57 minutes to complete the questions in the test, using a touch-screen to select your answers. The test is a set of 50 questions drawn from a bank of about 1,000, all of which have multiple-choice answers. In order to pass the test you must answer a minimum of 43 questions correctly within the given time. The Government may change the pass mark from time to time. Your driving school or the Driver & Vehicle Agency (DVA) will be able to tell you if there has been a change. The questions appear on the screen one at a time and you can return to any of the questions within the 57 minutes to re-check or alter your answers. The system will prompt you to return to any questions you have not answered fully.

Preparing for the Theory Test

You'll find that many of the theory questions relate directly to the Highway Code section of this book. Other useful reference books for this part of the test include the AA's *Theory Test,* which contains all of the official questions and answers from the DSA.

How to answer the questions

Each question has four, five or six possible answers. You must mark the boxes with the correct answer(s). Each question tells you how many answers to mark.

Study each question carefully, making sure you understand what it is asking you. Look carefully at any diagram, drawing or photograph. Before you look at the answer(s) given, decide what you think the correct answer(s) might be. You can then select the answer(s) that matches the one you had decided on. If you follow this system, you will avoid being confused by answers that appear to be similar.

What to expect in the Hazard Perception Test

After a break of up to three minutes you will begin the Hazard Perception part of the test. The Hazard Perception test lasts for about 20 minutes. Before you start you will be given some instructions explaining how the test works; you'll also get a chance to practise with the computer and mouse before you start.

Real road scenes feature in the film clips in the Hazard Perception test

Click the mouse when you spot potential hazards – the pedestrian crossing the side road and the cyclist approaching a parked vehicle (ringed in yellow). Click again as the hazard develops when the cyclist (ringed in red) moves out to overtake the parked vehicle

Next you will see 14 film clips of real street scenes with traffic such as cars, pedestrians, cyclists etc. The scenes are shot from the point of view of a driver in a car. You have to notice potential hazards that are developing on the road ahead – that is, problems that could lead to an accident.

As soon as you notice a hazard developing, click the mouse. A red flag will appear at the bottom of the screen to show that your response has been registered. You will have plenty of time to see the hazard but the sooner you notice it, the more marks you score.

Each clip has at least one hazard in it – some clips may have more than one hazard. You have to score a minimum of 44 out of 75 to pass, but the pass mark may change, so check with your instructor or the DVA before sitting your test. (Note that the computer has checks built in to show anyone trying to cheat – for example, someone who keeps clicking the mouse all the time.) Be aware that, unlike the Theory Test questions, you will not have an opportunity to go back to an earlier clip and change your response, so you need to concentrate throughout the test.

> **You have to pass both the Hazard Perception test and the Theory Test questions. At the end of the test you will be told your scores for both parts. Even if you failed on only one part of the Theory Test, you still have to take both parts again next time.**

Preparing for the Hazard Perception test

Who do you think have the most accidents – new or experienced drivers? New drivers have just had lessons, so they should remember how to drive safely, but in fact new drivers have the most accidents.

Learner drivers need training in how to spot hazards because they are often so busy thinking about the car's controls that they forget to watch the road and traffic – and losing concentration for even a second could prove fatal to you or another road user.

Proper training can help you to recognise more of the hazards that you will meet when driving and to spot those hazards earlier. So you are less likely to have an accident.

Your driving instructor has been trained to help you learn hazard perception skills and can give you plenty of practice in what to look out for when driving, how to anticipate hazards, and what action to take to deal with hazards of all kinds.

You won't be able to practise with the real film clips used in the test, of course, but training books and practice DVDs and videos are available.

THE PRACTICAL TEST

Once you have passed both parts of your Theory Test, you can apply for the Practical Test. The Practical Test is all about making sure that those who pass are competent and safe in the basic skills of driving.

> The requirements for passing your test are a combination of practical skills and mental understanding. The open road can be a risky environment, and your test result will show whether you're ready to go out there alone or whether you need a little more practice first.

> You'll be asked to sign a declaration that the insurance of your car is in order. Without this, the test can't proceed.

The paperwork

You'll need to have with you
- your Practical Test appointment letter
- Vehicle Registration Document
- MOT certificate (if applicable)
- your signed provisional driving licence (both parts if you've got a photo licence)
- your Theory Test pass certificate
- additional photographic identity (ID), if your licence doesn't have a photo

If your licence does not show your photograph, you must also bring with you a form of photographic identification, such as a current signed passport. A card such as a cheque guarantee or credit card, an employer's identity card, trade union card, but only if it is signed and has a photograph. For the full list of acceptable photographic ID, visit the Driver & Vehicle Agency website at www.dvani.gov.uk

Eyesight test

Your driving test begins with an eyesight test. You have to be able to read a normal number plate at a minimum distance of 20.5 metres (about 67.5 feet) or 20 metres (about 65.5 feet) for new-style number plates with smaller lettering. If you fail the eyesight test, your driving test will stop at that point and you will have failed.

Vehicle safety checks

You will have to answer two vehicle safety check questions. The questions fall into three categories
- identify…
- tell me how you would check…
- show me how you would check…

These questions are designed to make sure that you know how to check that your vehicle is safe to drive.

Although some checks may require you to identify where fluid levels should be checked you will not be asked to touch a hot engine or physically check fluid levels. You may refer to vehicle information systems (if fitted) when answering questions on fluid levels and tyre pressures.

All vehicles differ slightly so it is important that you get to know all the safety systems and engine layout in the vehicle in which you plan to take your practical test.

> **If you turn up for your test in an unsuitable vehicle, you will forfeit your test fee.**

The Driving Test
During the test you will be expected to drive for about 40 minutes along normal roads following the directions of the examiner. The roads are selected so as to provide a range of different conditions and road situations and a varied density of traffic.

Your examiner will select suitable areas for you to carry out the set exercises. He or she will tell you to pull up and stop, then he or she will explain the exercise to you before you do it
- you *will* be asked to perform and emergency stop, an angle start (move off from behind a parked car), and a number of normal starts (move off from the side of the road)
- you *will* be asked to perform two reversing exercises selected by the examiner from
  - reversing round a corner
  - reverse parking (behind a parked car, or into a marked bay)
  - turning in the road.

Throughout the test, the examiner will be assessing
- whether you are competent at controlling the car

- whether you are making normal progress for the roads you are on
- how you react to any hazards that occur in the course of the test
- whether you are noticing all traffic signs and signals and road markings, and reacting to them in the correct manner.

In order to pass the driving test, you must drive
- without committing any serious faults

or
- without committing more than 15 driving faults of a less serious nature.

If, during the test, you do not understand what the examiner says to you, ask him or her to repeat the instruction.

If you are faced with an unusually difficult or hazardous situation in the course of your test that results in you making a mistake, the examiner will take the circumstances into account when assessing you for that part of the test.

> **Driving test standards are monitored so that whatever examiner you get, or whatever test centre you go to, you should get the same result. You might find a senior officer in the car as well as the examiner; he or she is not watching you, but checking that the examiner is doing his or her job properly.**

How to prepare for the Practical Test

Be sure that you are ready to take the test. This is where choosing a reliable, qualified driving instructor is vital.

You should feel

- confident about driving in all conditions
- confident that you know the rules in this book
- confident that you can make decisions on your own about how to cope with hazards, without having to wait for your instructor to tell you what to do.

Driver's Record

Completing a Driver's Record (see example below) with your instructor should help you feel confident that you're ready to take your driving test.

The Driver's Record comes in two parts – one part for you and one for your instructor. It lists all the skills you need to master to become a safe driver and charts your progress in acquiring each of these skills through the following five levels:

1 Introduced
2 Under full instruction
3 Prompted
4 Seldom prompted
5 Independent

Take your copy of the Driver's Record to each lesson for your instructor to complete. It's also good practice to keep a separate record of driving experience gained when you are out driving with a friend or relative.

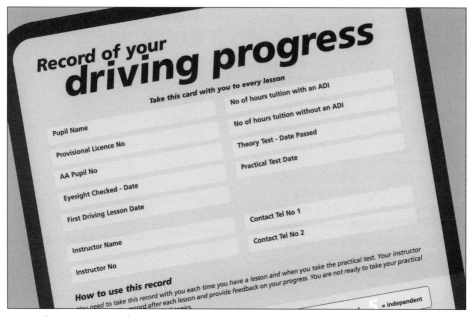

Record of your driving progress

Take this card with you to every lesson

Pupil Name

Provisional Licence No

AA Pupil No

Eyesight Checked - Date

First Driving Lesson Date

Instructor Name

Instructor No

No of hours tuition with an ADI

No of hours tuition without an ADI

Theory Test - Date Passed

Practical Test Date

Contact Tel No 1

Contact Tel No 2

How to use this record

You need to take this record with you each time you have a lesson and when you take the practical test. Your instructor ... record after each lesson and provide feedback on your progress. You are not ready to take your practical ...

5 = independent

A sample Driver's Record

Pages 110–112 (Annexe 3 – Motor vehicle documentation, learner and restricted driver requirements) lists some rules for newly qualified drivers in Northern Ireland. For example, after passing your driving test you must display amber R plates for 12 months and keep to a maximum speed limit of 45mph (72km/h). Annexe 8 (pages 122–123) is a safety code for new drivers.

When your instructor has completed all the boxes in your Driver's Record you are ready to take your test.

AFTER THE TEST

If you passed your test you'll be given a pass certificate, and a copy of the examiner's report showing any faults you made during your test. You'll find it useful to know where your weaknesses lie, so that you can concentrate on improving those aspects of your driving in the future.

With a full driving licence you are allowed to drive vehicles weighing up to 3.5 tonnes, use motorways for the first time, drive anywhere in the European Union and in many other countries worldwide, and to tow a small trailer. You are also on your own dealing with whatever circumstances may arise: fog, snow, ice, other drivers' mistakes. It is a huge responsibility. Driving on a motorway for the first time can be a daunting experience. A good driving school will offer you the option of a post-test motorway lesson with your own instructor, and it makes sense to take advantage of this.

If you failed you will naturally be disappointed, but it's not the end of the world – many people don't pass their first test, but then sail through a second or third, having built on the experience of what it's like to take a test. The examiner will give you a test report form, which is a record of all the skills assessed during the test, identifying any areas of weakness. He or she will also provide feedback in spoken form, and will explain to you which aspects of your driving still need improvement.

The Highway Code

Introduction

The Highway Code for Northern Ireland (hereafter referred to as *The Highway Code* or the Code) is essential reading for everyone.

The most vulnerable road users are pedestrians, particularly children, older or disabled people, cyclists, motorcyclists and horse riders. It is important that all road users are aware of the Code and are considerate towards each other. This applies to pedestrians as much as to drivers and riders.

Many of the rules in the Code are legal requirements, and if you disobey these rules you are committing a criminal offence. You may be fined, given penalty points on your licence or be disqualified from driving. In the most serious cases you may be sent to prison. Such rules are identified by the use of the words **'MUST/MUST NOT'**. In addition, each rule includes an abbreviated reference to the legislation that creates the offence. An explanation of the abbreviations is given in Annexe 4 – The road user and the law, on pages 113–114.

The Highway Code

Although failure to comply with the other rules of the Code will not, in itself, cause a person to be prosecuted, *The Highway Code* may be used in evidence in any court proceedings under the Traffic Legislation (see Annexe 4 – The road user and the law, pages 113–114) to establish liability. This includes rules that use advisory wording such as 'should/ should not' or 'do/do not'.

Knowing and applying the rules contained in *The Highway Code* could significantly reduce road casualties. Cutting the number of deaths and injuries that occur on our roads every day is a responsibility we all share. *The Highway Code* can help us discharge that responsibility. Further information on driving/riding techniques can be found in *The Official DSA Guide to Driving – the essential skills* and *The Official DSA Guide to Riding – the essential skills*.

The Highway Code is based on the Great Britain version. Although Northern Ireland road safety legislation continues to be brought into line with that in Great Britain, there are some differences that it has been necessary to reflect in this issue. For example, many Northern Ireland road users may not be familiar with equestrian and puffin crossings or trams. References to these issues have however been included as Northern Ireland residents who plan to visit Great Britain might find them helpful. It is recommended that anyone, especially drivers, intending to visit Great Britain should also purchase the Great Britain version of *The Highway Code*. It is also recommended that anyone intending to visit the Republic of Ireland should purchase a copy of *Rules of the Road* and note particularly that all speed limit signs in the Republic of Ireland relate to kilometres per hour. The Great Britain Highway Code is available online at www.direct.gov.uk under travel and transport. The Republic of Ireland *Rules of the Road* is available at www.rulesoftheroad.ie.

Rules for pedestrians

General guidance

1. Footways or footpaths (including any path along the side of a road) should be used if provided. Where possible, avoid being next to the kerb with your back to the traffic. If you have to step into the road, look both ways first. Always show care and consideration for others.

2. If there is no footway or footpath walk on the right-hand side of the road so that you can see oncoming traffic. You should take extra care and
- be prepared to walk in single file, especially on narrow roads or in poor light
- keep close to the side of the road.

It may be safer to cross the road well before a sharp right-hand bend so that oncoming traffic has a better chance of seeing you. Cross back after the bend.

3. Help other road users to see you. Wear or carry something light-coloured, bright or fluorescent in poor daylight conditions. When it is dark, use reflective materials (e.g. armbands, sashes, waistcoats, jackets, footwear), which can be seen by drivers using headlights up to three times as far away as non-reflective materials.

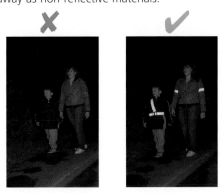

Help yourself to be seen

4. Young children should not be out alone on the footway, footpath or road (see Rule 7). When taking children out, keep between them and the traffic and hold their hands firmly. Strap very young children into pushchairs or use reins. When pushing a young child in a buggy, do not push the buggy into the road when checking to see if it is clear to cross, particularly from between parked vehicles.

5. Organised walks. Large groups of people walking together should use a footway or footpath if available; if one is not, they should keep to the left. Look-outs should be positioned at the front and back of the group, and they should wear fluorescent clothes in daylight and reflective clothes in the dark. At night, the look-out in front should show a white light and the one at the back a red light. People on the outside of large groups should also carry lights and wear reflective clothing.

6. Motorways. Pedestrians MUST NOT be on motorways or slip roads except in an emergency (see Rules 271 and 275).

Law RO Art 20 & MTR reg 13(1)(b)

Crossing the road

7. The Green Cross Code. The advice given below on crossing the road is for all pedestrians. Children should be taught the Code and should not be allowed out alone until they can understand and use it properly. The age when they can do this is different for each child. Many children cannot judge how fast vehicles are going or how far away they are. Children learn by example, so parents and carers should always use the Code in full when out with their children. They are responsible for deciding at what age children can use it safely by themselves.

a. First find a safe place to cross and where there is space to reach the footway or footpath on the other side. Where there is a crossing nearby, use it. It is safer to cross using a subway, a footbridge, an island, a zebra, pelican, toucan or puffin crossing, or where there is a crossing point controlled by a police officer or a school crossing patrol. Otherwise choose a place where you can see clearly in all directions. Try to avoid crossing between parked cars (see Rule 14), on a blind bend, or close to the brow of a hill. Move to a space where drivers and riders can see you clearly. Do not cross the road diagonally.

Look all around and listen for traffic before crossing

b. Stop just before you get to the kerb, where you can see if anything is coming. Do not get too close to the traffic. If there's no footway or footpath, keep back from the edge of the road but make sure you can still see approaching traffic.

c. Look all around for traffic and listen. Traffic could come from any direction. Listen as well, because you can sometimes hear traffic before you see it.

d. If traffic is coming, let it pass. Look all around again and listen. Do not cross until there is a safe gap in the traffic and you are certain that there is plenty of time. Remember, even if traffic is a long way off, it may be approaching very quickly.

e. When it is safe, go straight across the road – do not run. Keep looking and listening for traffic while you cross, in case there is any traffic you did not see, or in case other traffic appears suddenly. Look out for cyclists and motorcyclists travelling between lanes of traffic. Do not walk diagonally across the road.

8. At a junction. When crossing the road, look out for traffic turning into the road, especially from behind you. If you have started crossing and traffic wants to turn into the road, you have priority and they should give way (see Rule 170).

9. Pedestrian safety barriers. Where there are barriers, cross the road only at the gaps provided for pedestrians. Do not climb over the barriers or walk between them and the road.

10. Tactile paving. Raised surfaces that can be felt underfoot provide warning and guidance to blind or partially sighted people. The most common surfaces are a series of raised studs, which are used at crossing points with a dropped kerb, or a series of rounded raised bars which are used at level crossings, at the top and bottom of steps and at some other hazards.

11. One-way streets. Check which way the traffic is moving. Do not cross until it is safe to do so without stopping. Bus and cycle lanes may operate in the opposite direction to the rest of the traffic.

12. Bus and cycle lanes. Take care when crossing these lanes as traffic may be moving faster than in the other lanes, or against the flow of traffic.

13. Routes shared with cyclists. Some cycle tracks run alongside footways or footpaths, using a segregating feature to separate cyclists from people on foot. Segregated routes may also incorporate short lengths of tactile paving to help visually impaired people stay on the correct side. On the pedestrian side this will comprise a series of flat-topped bars running across the direction of travel (ladder pattern). On the cyclist side the same bars are orientated in the direction of travel (tramline pattern). Not all routes which are shared with cyclists are segregated. Take extra care where this is so (see Rule 62).

14. Parked vehicles. If you have to cross between parked vehicles, use the outside edges of the vehicles as if they were the kerb. Stop there and make sure you can see all around and that the traffic can see you. Make sure there is a gap between any parked vehicles on the other side, so you can reach the footway or footpath. Never cross the road in front of, or behind, any vehicle with its engine running, especially a large vehicle, as the driver may not be able to see you.

15. Reversing vehicles. Never cross behind a vehicle which is reversing, showing white reversing lights or sounding a warning.

16. Moving vehicles. You **MUST NOT** get onto or hold onto a moving vehicle.
Law RTO 1995 Art 37

17. At night. Wear something reflective to make it easier for others to see you (see Rule 3). If there is no pedestrian crossing nearby, cross the road near a street light so that traffic can see you more easily.

Crossings
18. At all crossings. When using any type of crossing you should
- always check that the traffic has stopped before you start to cross or push a pram onto a crossing
- always cross between the studs or over the zebra markings. Do not cross at the side of the crossing or on the zig-zag lines, as it can be dangerous.

You **MUST NOT** loiter on any type of crossing.
Laws RTRO Art 59(4) & PCR reg 17

19. Zebra crossings. Give traffic plenty of time to see you and to stop before you start to cross. Vehicles will need more time when the road is slippery. Wait until traffic has stopped from both directions or the road is clear before crossing. Remember that traffic does not have to stop until someone has moved onto the crossing. Keep looking both ways, and listening, in case a driver or rider has not seen you and attempts to overtake a vehicle that has stopped.

Zebra crossings have flashing beacons

20. Where there is an island in the middle of a zebra crossing, wait on the island and follow Rule 19 before you cross the second half of the road – it is a separate crossing.

Zebra crossings with a central island are two separate crossings

21. At traffic lights. There may be special signals for pedestrians. You should only start to cross the road when the green figure shows. If you have started to cross the road and the green figure goes out, you should still have time to reach the other side, but do not delay. If no pedestrian signals have been provided, watch carefully and do not cross until the traffic lights are red and the traffic has stopped. Keep looking and check for traffic that may be turning the corner. Remember that traffic lights may let traffic move in some lanes while traffic in other lanes has stopped.

At traffic lights, puffin and pelican crossings
*At pelican crossings only

22. Pelican crossings. These are signal-controlled crossings operated by pedestrians. Push the control button to activate the traffic signals. When the red figure shows, do not cross. When a steady green figure shows, check the traffic has stopped then cross with care. When the green figure begins to flash you should not cross. If you have already started you should have time to finish crossing safely.

23. Puffin crossings differ from pelican crossings as the red and green figures are above the control box on your side of the road and there is no flashing green figure phase. Press the button and wait for the green figure to show.

24. When the road is congested, traffic on your side of the road may be forced to stop even though their lights are green. Traffic may still be moving on the other side of the road, so press the button and wait for the signal to cross.

25. Toucan crossings are light-controlled crossings which allow cyclists and pedestrians to share crossing space and cross at the same time. They are push-button operated. Cyclists are permitted to ride across.

Toucan crossings can be used by both cyclists and pedestrians

26. At some crossings there is a bleeping sound or voice signal to indicate to blind or partially sighted people when the steady green figure is showing, and there may be a tactile signal to help deafblind people.

27. Equestrian crossings are for horse riders. They have pavement barriers, wider crossing spaces, horse and rider figures in the light panels and either two sets of controls (one higher), or just one higher control panel.

Equestrian crossings are used by horse riders.
There is often a parallel crossing

28. 'Staggered' pelican or puffin crossings. When the crossings on each side of the central refuge are not in line they are two separate crossings. On reaching the central island, press the button again and wait for a steady green figure.

Staggered crossings (with an island in the middle)
are two separate crossings

29. Crossings controlled by an authorised person. Do not cross the road unless you are signalled to do so by a police officer or school crossing patrol. Always cross in front of them.

30. Where there are no controlled crossing points available it is advisable to cross where there is an island in the middle of the road. Use the Green Cross Code (see Rule 7) to cross to the island then stop and use it again to cross the second half of the road.

Situations needing extra care

31. Emergency vehicles. If an ambulance, fire engine, police or any other emergency vehicle approaches using flashing blue lights, headlights and/or sirens, keep off the road.

32. Buses. Get on or off a bus only when it has stopped to allow you to do so. Watch out for cyclists when you are getting off. Never cross the road directly behind or in front of a bus. Wait until it has moved off and you can see the road clearly in both directions.

33. Tramways. These may run through pedestrian areas. Their path will be marked out by shallow kerbs, changes in the paving or other road surface, white lines or yellow dots. Cross at designated crossings where provided. Elsewhere treat trams as you would other vehicles and look both ways along the track before crossing. Do not walk along the track as trams may come up behind you. Trams move quietly and cannot steer to avoid you.

34. Railway level crossings. You **MUST NOT** cross or pass a stop line when the red lights show (including a red pedestrian figure). Also do not cross if an alarm is sounding or the barriers are being lowered. The tone of the alarm may change if another train is approaching. If there are no lights, alarms or barriers, stop, look both ways and listen before crossing. A tactile surface comprising rounded bars running across the direction of pedestrian travel may be installed on the footway or footpath approaching a level crossing to warn visually impaired people of its presence. The tactile surface should extend across the full width of the footway or footpath and should be located at an appropriate distance from the barrier or projected line of the barrier.
Law TSR reg 39

35. Street, footway and footpath repairs. A footway or footpath may be closed temporarily because it is not safe to use. Take extra care if you are directed to walk on or to cross the road.

Rules for users of powered wheelchairs and powered mobility scooters

(Called Invalid Carriages in law)

36. There is one class of manual wheelchair (called a Class 1 Invalid Carriage) and two classes of powered wheelchairs and powered mobility scooters. Manual wheelchairs and Class 2 vehicles are those with an upper speed limit of 4mph (6km/h) and are designed to be used on footways or footpaths. Class 3 vehicles are those with an upper speed limit of 8mph (12km/h) and are equipped to be used on the road as well as footways or footpaths.

37. When you are on the road you should obey the guidance and rules for other vehicles; when on the footway or footpath you should follow the guidance and rules for pedestrians.

On footways or footpaths

38. Footways or footpaths are safer than roads and should be used when available. You should give pedestrians priority and show consideration for other footway or footpath users, particularly those with a hearing or visual impairment who may not be aware that you are there.

39. Powered wheelchairs and scooters **MUST NOT** travel faster than 4mph (6km/h) on footways or footpaths or in pedestrian areas. You may need to reduce your speed to adjust to other footway or footpath users who may not be able to move out of your way quickly enough or where the footway or footpath is too narrow.

Law MV(IC)R reg 4

40. When moving off the footway or footpath onto the road, you should take special care. Before moving off, always look round and make sure it's safe to join the traffic. Always try to use dropped kerbs when moving off the footway or footpath, even if this means travelling further to locate one.If you have to climb or descend a kerb, always approach it at right angles and don't try to negotiate a kerb higher than the vehicle manufacturer's recommendations.

On the road

41. You should take care when travelling on the road as you may be travelling more slowly than other traffic (your machine is restricted to 8mph [12km/h] and may be less visible).

The Highway Code

42. When on the road, Class 3 vehicles should travel in the direction of the traffic. Class 2 users should always use the footway or footpath when it is available. When there is no footway or footpath, you should use caution when on the road. Class 2 users should, where possible, travel in the direction of the traffic as this is safer. If you are travelling at night, when lights **MUST** be used, you should travel in the direction of the traffic to avoid confusing other road users.
Law MV(IC)R reg 9

43. You **MUST** follow the same rules about using lights, indicators and horns as for other road vehicles, if your vehicle is fitted with them. At night, lights **MUST** be used. Be aware that other road users may not be able to see you and you should make yourself more visible – even in the daytime and also at dusk – by, for instance, wearing a reflective jacket or reflective strips on the back of the vehicle.
Law MV(IC)R reg 9

44. Take extra care at road junctions. When going straight ahead, check to make sure there are no vehicles about to cross your path from the left, the right, or overtaking you and turning left. There are several options for dealing with right turns, especially turning from a major road. If moving into the middle of the road is difficult or dangerous, you can
* stop on the left-hand side of the road and wait for a safe gap in the traffic
* negotiate the turn as a pedestrian, i.e. travel along the footway or footpath and cross the road between the footways or footpaths where it is safe to do so. Class 3 users should switch the vehicle to the lower speed limit when on footways or footpaths.
If the junction is too hazardous, it may be worth considering an alternative route. Similarly, when negotiating major roundabouts (i.e. with two or more lanes) it may be safer for you to use the footway or footpath or find a route which avoids the roundabout altogether.

45. All normal parking restrictions should be observed. Your vehicle should not be left unattended if it causes an obstruction to other pedestrians – especially those in wheelchairs. Parking concessions provided under the Blue Badge scheme (see Further reading, page 125) will apply to those vehicles displaying a valid badge.

46. These vehicles **MUST NOT** be used on motorways (see Rule 253). They should not be used on unrestricted dual carriageways where the speed limit exceeds 50mph (80km/h) but if they are used on these dual carriageways, they **MUST** have a flashing amber beacon. A flashing amber beacon should be used on all other dual carriageways (see Rule 220).
Laws RO Art 20(1), (3) & (4), RVLR regs 20(1) & 29

Rules about animals

Horse-drawn vehicles

47. Horse-drawn vehicles used on the road should be operated and maintained in accordance with standards set out in the Department for Transport's Code of Practice for Horse-Drawn Vehicles. This Code lays down the requirements for a road driving assessment in Great Britain and includes a comprehensive list of safety checks to ensure that a carriage and its fittings are safe and in good working order.

48. Safety equipment and clothing. All horse-drawn vehicles should have two red rear reflectors. It is safer not to drive at night but if you do, a light showing white to the front and red to the rear **MUST** be fitted.
Law RVLR reg 4

Horse riders

49. Safety equipment. Children under the age of 14 **MUST** wear a helmet which complies with the Regulations. It **MUST** be fastened securely. Other riders should also follow these requirements. These requirements do not apply to a child who is a follower of the Sikh religion while wearing a turban.
Laws H(PHYR)O Art 3 & H(PHYR)R

50. Other clothing. You should wear
- boots or shoes with hard soles and heels
- light-coloured or fluorescent clothing in daylight
- reflective clothing if you have to ride at night or in poor visibility.

Help yourself to be seen

51. At night. It is safer not to ride on the road at night or in poor visibility, but if you do, make sure your horse has reflective bands above the fetlock joints. A light which shows white to the front and red to the rear should be fitted, with a band, to the rider's right arm and/or leg/riding boot. If you are leading a horse at night, carry a light in your right hand, showing white to the front and red to the rear, and make sure both you and your horse are wearing reflective garments . It is strongly recommended that a fluorescent/reflective tail guard is also worn by your horse.

Riding

52. Before you take a horse onto a road, you should
- ensure all tack fits well and is in good condition
- make sure you can control the horse.

Always ride with other, less nervous horses if you think that your horse will be nervous of traffic. Never ride a horse without both a saddle and bridle.

53. Before riding off or turning, look behind you to make sure it is safe, then give a clear arm signal.
When riding on the road you should
- keep to the left
- keep both hands on the reins unless you are signalling
- keep both feet in the stirrups
- not carry another person
- not carry anything which might affect your balance or get tangled up with the reins
- keep a horse you are leading to your left
- move in the direction of the traffic flow in a one-way street
- never ride more than two abreast, and ride in single file on narrow or busy roads and when riding round bends.

54. You should not take a horse onto a footway, footpath or cycle track. In Great Britain, use a bridleway where possible. In Great Britain, equestrian crossings may be provided for horse riders to cross the road and you should use these where available (see Rule 27). You should dismount at level crossings where a 'horse rider dismount' sign is displayed.

55. Avoid roundabouts wherever possible. If you use them you should
- keep to the left and watch out for vehicles crossing your path to leave or join the roundabout
- signal right when riding across exits to show you are not leaving
- signal left just before you leave the roundabout.

Other animals

56. Dogs. Do not let a dog out on the road on its own. Keep it on a short lead when walking on the footway, footpath, road or path shared with cyclists or horse riders.

57. When in a vehicle, make sure dogs and other animals are suitably restrained so they cannot distract you while you are driving or injure you, or themselves, if you stop quickly. A seat belt harness, pet carrier, dog cage or dog guard are ways of restraining animals in cars.

58. Animals being herded. These should be kept under control at all times. You should, if possible, send another person along the road in front to warn other road users, especially at a bend or the brow of a hill. It is safer not to move animals after dark, but if you do, then wear reflective clothing and ensure that lights are carried (white at the front and red at the rear of the herd).

Rules for cyclists

These rules are in addition to those in the following sections, which apply to all vehicles (except the Motorways section, page 79). See also Annexe 1 – You and your bicycle, page 108.

59. Clothing. You should wear in the correct size and securely fastened
- a cycle helmet which conforms to current regulations
- appropriate clothes for cycling. Avoid clothes that may get tangled in the chain, or in a wheel or may obscure your lights
- light-coloured or fluorescent clothing which helps other road users to see you in daylight and poor light
- reflective clothing and/or accessories (belt, arm or ankle bands) in the dark.

Help yourself to be seen

60. Between sunset and sunrise your cycle MUST have white front and red rear lights lit. It MUST also be fitted with a red rear reflector (and amber pedal reflectors, if manufactured after 24 January 1996). White front reflectors and spoke reflectors will also help you to be seen. Flashing lights are permitted but it is recommended that cyclists who are riding in areas without street lighting use a steady front lamp.
Law RVLR regs 13, 15, 21 & 27 (as amended by RVL(A)R)

When cycling
61. Cycle routes and other facilities. Use cycle routes, advanced stop lines, cycle boxes and toucan crossings unless at the time it is unsafe to do so. Use of these facilities is not compulsory and will depend on your experience and skills, but they can make your journey safer.

62. Cycle tracks. These are normally located away from the road, but may also be found alongside footways or footpaths. Cyclists and pedestrians may be segregated or they may share the same space (unsegregated). When using segregated tracks you **MUST** keep to the side intended for cyclists as the pedestrian side remains a footway or footpath. Take care when passing pedestrians, especially children, older or disabled people, and allow them plenty of room. Always be prepared to slow down and stop if necessary. Take care near road junctions as you may have difficulty seeing other road users, who might not notice you.
Law RTRO Arts 3 & 4(5)

63. Cycle lanes. These are marked by a white line (which may be broken) along the carriageway (see Rule 140). When using a cycle lane, keep within the lane when practicable. Before leaving a cycle lane check that it is safe to do so and signal your intention clearly to other road users. Use of cycle lanes is not compulsory and will depend on your experience and skills, but they can make your journey safer.

64. You **MUST NOT** cycle on a footway or footpath unless on a cycle track where one has been provided.
Law RTRO Art 3

65. Bus Lanes. Most bus lanes, excluding motorway bus lanes, may be used by motorcyclists and cyclists as indicated on signs. Watch out for people getting on or off a bus. Be very careful when overtaking a bus or leaving a bus lane as you will be entering a busier traffic flow.

66. You should
• keep both hands on the handlebars except when signalling or changing gear
• keep both feet on the pedals
• never ride more than two abreast, and ride in single file on narrow or busy roads and when riding round bends
• not ride close behind another vehicle
• not carry anything that will affect your balance or may get tangled up with your wheels or chain
• be considerate of other road users, particularly blind and partially sighted pedestrians. Let them know you are there when necessary, for example by sounding your bell or horn.

The Highway Code

67. You should
- look all around before moving away from the kerb, turning or manoeuvring, to make sure it is safe to do so. Give a clear signal to show other road users what you intend to do (see Signals to other road users, page 93)
- look well ahead for obstructions in the road, such as drains, pot-holes and parked vehicles so that you do not have to swerve suddenly to avoid them. Leave plenty of room when passing parked vehicles and watch out for doors being opened or pedestrians stepping into your path
- be aware of traffic coming up behind you
- take extra care near road humps, narrowings and other traffic calming features
- take care when overtaking (see Rules 162–169).

68. You **MUST NOT**
- carry a passenger unless your cycle has been built or adapted to carry one
- hold onto a moving vehicle or trailer
- ride in a dangerous, careless or inconsiderate manner
- ride when under the influence of drink or drugs, including medicine.

Law RTO 1995 Arts 35, 37, 42, 43 & 44

69. You **MUST** obey all traffic signs and traffic light signals.

Laws RTO 1995 Art 50, TSR reg 8

70. When parking your cycle
- find a conspicuous location where it can be seen by passers-by
- use cycle stands or other cycle parking facilities wherever possible
- do not leave it where it would cause an obstruction or hazard to other road users
- secure it well so that it will not fall over and become an obstruction or hazard.

71. You **MUST NOT** cross the stop line when the traffic lights are red. Some junctions have an advanced stop line to enable you to wait and position yourself ahead of other traffic (see Rule 178).

Laws RTO 1995 Art 50 & TSR reg 33(1)

Road junctions

72. On the left. When approaching a junction on the left, watch out for vehicles turning in front of you, out of or into the side road. Just before you turn, check for undertaking cyclists or motorcyclists. Do not ride on the inside of vehicles signalling or slowing down to turn left.

73. Pay particular attention to long vehicles, which need a lot of room to manoeuvre at corners. Be aware that drivers may not see you. They may have to move over to the right before turning left. Wait until they have completed the manoeuvre because the rear wheels come very close to the kerb while turning. Do not be tempted to ride in the space between them and the kerb.

74. On the right. If you are turning right, check the traffic to ensure it is safe, then signal and move to the centre of the road. Wait until there is a safe gap in the oncoming traffic before completing the turn. It may be safer to wait on the left until there is a safe gap or to dismount and push your cycle across the road.

75. Dual carriageways. Remember that traffic on most dual carriageways moves quickly. When crossing, wait for a safe gap and cross each carriageway in turn. Take extra care when crossing slip roads.

Roundabouts

76. Full details about the correct procedure at roundabouts are contained in Rules 184–190 and in the Appendix on pages 126–129. Roundabouts can be hazardous and should be approached with care.

77. You may feel safer walking your cycle round on the footway, footpath or verge. If you decide to keep to the left you should
- be aware that drivers may not easily see you
- take extra care when cycling across exits. You may need to signal right to show you are not leaving the roundabout
- watch out for vehicles crossing your path to leave or join the roundabout.

78. Give plenty of room to long vehicles on the roundabout as they need more space to manoeuvre. Do not ride in the space they need to get round the roundabout. It may be safer to wait until they have cleared the roundabout.

Crossing the road

79. Do not ride across equestrian crossings, as they are for horse riders only. Do not ride across a pelican, puffin or zebra crossing. Dismount and wheel your cycle across.

80. Toucan crossings. These are light-controlled crossings, which allow cyclists and pedestrians to share crossing space and cross at the same time. They are push-button operated. Pedestrians and cyclists will see the green signal together. Cyclists are permitted to ride across.

81. Cycle-only crossings. Cycle tracks on opposite sides of the road may be linked by signalled crossings. You may ride across but you **MUST NOT** cross until the green cycle symbol is showing.
Law TSR reg 33(1)

82. Level crossings/tramways. Take extra care when crossing the tracks (see Rule 306). You should dismount at level crossings where a 'cyclist dismount' sign is displayed.

Rules for motorcyclists

These rules are in addition to those in the following sections, which apply to all vehicles. For motorcycle licence requirements see Annexe 2, pages 108–109.

General

83. On all journeys, the rider and pillion passenger on a motorcycle, scooter or moped **MUST** wear a protective helmet. This does not apply to a follower of the Sikh religion while wearing a turban. Helmets **MUST** comply with the Regulations and they **MUST** be fastened securely. Riders and passengers of motor tricycles and quadricycles, also called quadbikes, should also wear a protective helmet. Before each journey check that your helmet visor is clean and in good condition.

Laws MC(PH)R (as amended) reg 2, RTO 1995 Arts 27 & 28

84. It is also advisable to wear eye protectors, which **MUST** comply with the Regulations. Scratched or poorly fitting eye protectors can limit your view when riding, particularly in bright sunshine and the hours of darkness. Consider wearing ear protection. Strong boots, gloves and suitable clothing may help to protect you if you are involved in a collision.

Laws MC(EP)R (as amended) reg 2 & RTO 1995 Art 29

85. You **MUST NOT** carry more than one pillion passenger, who **MUST** sit astride the machine on a proper seat. They should face forward with both feet on the footrests. You **MUST NOT** carry a pillion passenger unless your motorcycle is designed to do so. Provisional licence holders **MUST NOT** carry a pillion passenger.

Laws RTO 1995 Art 34, MV(DL)R reg 12(5) & CUR reg 118

86. Daylight riding. Make yourself as visible as possible from the side as well as the front and rear. You could wear a light or brightly coloured helmet and fluorescent clothing or strips. Dipped headlights, even in good daylight, may also make you more conspicuous. However, be aware that other vehicle drivers may still not have seen you, or judged your distance or speed correctly, especially at junctions.

Help yourself to be seen

87. Riding in the dark. Wear reflective clothing or strips to improve your visibility in the dark. These reflect light from the headlamps of other vehicles, making you visible from a longer distance. See Rules 113–116 for lighting requirements.

88. Manoeuvring. You should be aware of what is behind and to the sides before manoeuvring. Look behind you; use mirrors if they are fitted. When in traffic queues, look out for pedestrians crossing between vehicles and vehicles emerging from junctions or changing lanes. Position yourself so that drivers in front can see you in their mirrors. Additionally, when filtering in slow-moving traffic, take care and keep your speed low.
Remember: Observation – Signal – Manoeuvre.

Rules for drivers and motorcyclists

89. Vehicle condition. You **MUST** ensure your vehicle and trailer comply with the full requirements of the Motor Vehicles (Construction and Use) Regulations (NI) and the Road Vehicles Lighting Regulations (NI) (see Annexe 4 – The road user and the law, pages 113–114).
Laws CUR, RVLR

Fitness to drive

90. Make sure that you are fit to drive. You **MUST** report to the Driver and Vehicle Agency any health condition likely to affect your driving.
Law RTO 1981 Art 11

91. Driving when you are tired greatly increases your risk of collision. To minimise this risk
- make sure you are fit to drive. Do not begin a journey if you are tired. Get a good night's sleep before embarking on a long journey
- avoid undertaking long journeys between midnight and 6am, when natural alertness is at a minimum
- plan your journey to take sufficient breaks. A minimum break of at least 15 minutes after every two hours of driving is recommended
- if you feel at all sleepy, stop in a safe place. Do not stop on the hard shoulder of a motorway
- the most effective ways to counter sleepiness are to drink, for example, two cups of caffeinated coffee and to take a short nap (at least 15 minutes).

92. Vision. You **MUST** be able to read a vehicle number plate, in good daylight, from a distance of 20 metres (or 20.5 metres where the old-style number plate is used). If you need to wear glasses (or contact lenses) to do this, you **MUST** wear them at all times while driving. The police have the power to require a driver to undertake an eyesight test.
Laws RTO 1981 Art 154, MV(DL)R reg 29 & sch 7 & MVDL(A)R

93. Slow down, and if necessary stop, if you are dazzled by bright sunlight.

94. At night or in poor visibility, do not use tinted glasses, lenses or visors if they restrict your vision.

Alcohol and drugs

95. Do not drink and drive as it will seriously affect your judgement and abilities. You **MUST NOT** drive with a breath alcohol level higher than 35 microgrammes/100 millilitres of breath or a blood alcohol level of more than 80 milligrammes/100 millilitres of blood. Alcohol will
- give a false sense of confidence
- reduce co-ordination and slow down reactions
- affect judgement of speed, distance and risk
- reduce your driving ability, even if you're below the legal limit
- take time to leave your body; you may be unfit to drive in the evening after drinking at lunchtime, or in the morning after drinking the previous evening.

The best solution is not to drink at all when driving, because any amount of alcohol can impair your driving ability. If you are going to drink, arrange another means of transport.

Law RTO 1995 Arts 13, 15 & 16

96. You **MUST NOT** drive under the influence of drugs or medicine. Check the instructions or ask your doctor or pharmacist. Using illegal drugs is highly dangerous. Never take them if you intend to drive; the effects are unpredictable, but can be even more severe than alcohol and may result in fatal or serious road crashes.

Law RTO 1995 Art 15

97. Before setting off. You should ensure that
- you have planned your route and allowed sufficient time
- clothing and footwear do not prevent you using the controls in the correct manner
- you know where all the controls are and how to use them before you need them. Not all vehicles are the same; do not wait until it is too late to find out
- your mirrors and seat are adjusted correctly to ensure comfort, full control and maximum vision
- head restraints are properly adjusted to reduce the risk of neck and spine injuries in the event of a collision
- you have sufficient fuel before commencing your journey, especially if it includes motorway driving. It can be dangerous to lose power when driving in traffic
- your vehicle is legal and roadworthy
- you have switched off your mobile phone.

Make sure head restraints are properly adjusted

98. Vehicle towing and loading. As a driver

- you **MUST NOT** tow more than your licence permits. If you passed a car test after 1 January 1997 you are restricted on the weight of trailer you can tow
- you **MUST NOT** overload your vehicle or trailer. You should not tow a weight greater than that recommended by the manufacturer of your vehicle
- you **MUST** secure your load and it **MUST NOT** stick out dangerously. Make sure any heavy or sharp objects and any animals are secured safely. If there is a collision, they might hit someone inside the vehicle and cause serious injury
- you should properly distribute the weight in your caravan or trailer, with heavy items mainly over the axle(s) and ensure a downward load on the tow ball. Manufacturer's recommended weight and tow ball load should not be exceeded. This should avoid the possibility of swerving or snaking and going out of control. If this does happen, ease off the accelerator and reduce speed gently to regain control
- carrying a load or pulling a trailer may require you to adjust the headlights.

In the event of a breakdown, be aware that towing a vehicle on a tow rope is potentially dangerous. You should consider professional recovery.

Laws CUR reg 115 & MV(DL)R reg 32

The Highway Code

Seat belts and child restraints

99. You MUST wear a seat belt in cars, vans and other goods vehicles if one is fitted (see table below). Adults, and children aged 14 years and over, MUST use a seat belt where fitted, when seated in minibuses, buses and coaches. Exemptions are allowed for the holders of medical exemption certificates and those making deliveries or collections in goods vehicles when travelling less than 50 metres (approx. 162 feet).
Laws RTO 1995 Arts 23 & 24, RTO 2007 Art 26, MV(WSB)R & MV(WSBCFS)R & MV(WSB)(A) R

Seat Belt Requirements
This table summarises the main legal requirements for wearing seat belts in cars, vans and other goods vehicles

	Front seat	Rear seat	Who is responsible?
Driver	Seat belt MUST be worn if fitted		Driver
Child under 3 years of age	Correct child restraint MUST be used	Correct child restraint MUST be used. If one is not available in a taxi, may travel unrestrained.	Driver
Child from 3rd birthday up to 1.35 metres (approx 4ft 5ins) in height (or 12th birthday, whichever they reach first)	Correct child restraint MUST be used	Correct child restraint MUST be used where seat belts fitted. MUST use adult belt if correct child restraint is not available in a licensed taxi or private hire vehicle, or for reasons of unexpected necessity over a short distance, or if two occupied restraints prevent fitment of a third.	Driver
Child over 1.35 metres (approx 4ft 5ins) in height or 12 or 13 years	Seat belt MUST be worn if available	Seat belt MUST be worn if available	Driver
Adult passengers aged 14 and over	Seat belt MUST be worn if available	Seat belt MUST be worn if available	Passenger

100. The driver **MUST** ensure that all children under 14 years of age in cars, vans and other goods vehicles wear seat belts or sit in an approved child restraint where required (see table opposite). If a child is under 1.35 metres (approx 4 feet 5 inches) tall, a baby seat, child seat, booster seat or booster cushion suitable for the child's weight and fitted to the manufacturer's instructions **MUST** be used.

Laws RTO 1995 Arts 23 & 24, MV(WSB)R & MV(WSBCFS)R & MV(WSB)(A)R

Make sure that a child uses a suitable restraint which is correctly adjusted

101. A rear-facing baby seat **MUST NOT** be fitted into a seat protected by an active frontal airbag, as in a crash it can cause serious injury or death to the child.

Laws RTO 1995 Arts 23 & 24, MV(WSB)R & MV(WSBCFS)R & MV(WSB)(A)R

102. Children in cars, vans and other goods vehicles. Drivers who are carrying children in cars, vans and other goods vehicles should also ensure that

- children should get into the vehicle through the door nearest the kerb
- child restraints are properly fitted to manufacturer's instructions
- children do not sit behind the rear seats in an estate car or hatchback, unless a special child seat has been fitted
- the child safety door locks, where fitted, are used when children are in the vehicle
- children are kept under control.

General rules, techniques and advice for all drivers and riders

This section should be read by all drivers, motorcyclists, cyclists and horse riders. The rules in *The Highway Code* do not give you the right of way in any circumstance, but they advise you when you should give way to others. Always give way if it can help to avoid an incident.

Signals

103. Signals warn and inform other road users, including pedestrians (see Signals to other road users, page 93), of your intended actions. You should always
- give clear signals in plenty of time, having checked it is not misleading to signal at that time
- use them to advise other road users before changing course or direction, stopping or moving off
- cancel them after use
- make sure your signals will not confuse others. If, for instance, you want to stop after a side road, do not signal until you are passing the road. If you signal earlier it may give the impression that you intend to turn into the road. Your brake lights will warn traffic behind you that you are slowing down
- use an arm signal to emphasise or reinforce your signal if necessary. Remember that signalling does not give you priority.

104. You should also
- watch out for signals given by other road users and proceed only when you are satisfied that it is safe
- be aware that an indicator on another vehicle may not have been cancelled.

105. You **MUST** obey signals given by police officers and Driver and Vehicle Agency Enforcement Officers (see Signals by authorised persons, pages 94–95) and signs used by school crossing patrols.
Laws RTRO Art 60, RTO 1995 Arts 49, 75 & 76 & RTO 1981 Arts 180 and 180A

106. Police stopping procedures. If police in a vehicle want to stop your vehicle they will, where possible, attract your attention by
- flashing blue lights or headlights or sounding their siren or horn, usually from behind
- directing you to pull over to the side by pointing and/or using the left indicator.

You **MUST** then pull over and stop as soon as it is safe to do so. Then switch off your engine.
Law RTO 1981 Art 180

Other stopping procedures

107. Driver and Vehicle Agency Enforcement Officers have powers to stop vehicles on all roads, including motorways. They will attract your attention by flashing amber lights
- either from the front requesting you to follow them to a safe place to stop
- or from behind directing you to pull over to the side by pointing and/or using the left indicator.

It is an offence not to comply with their directions. You **MUST** obey any signals given (see Signals by authorised persons, pages 94–95).

Law RTO 1981 Art 180A

108. Highways Agency Traffic Officers have powers to stop vehicles on most motorways and some 'A' class roads in England only. If HA traffic officers in uniform want to stop your vehicle on safety grounds (e.g. an insecure load) they will, where possible, attract your attention by
- flashing amber lights, usually from behind
- directing you to pull over to the side by pointing and/or using the left indicator.

You **MUST** then pull over and stop as soon as it is safe to do so.
Then switch off your engine. It is an offence not to comply with their directions (see Signals by authorised persons, pages 94–95).

Law RTA 1988, sects 35 & 163 as amended by TMA 2004, sect 6

109. Traffic light signals and traffic signs. You **MUST** obey all traffic light signals (see Light signals controlling traffic, page 92) and traffic signs giving orders, including temporary signals and signs (see Signs giving orders, Warning signs and Direction signs, pages 96–101). Make sure you know, understand and act on all other traffic and information signs and road markings (see Signs giving orders, Warning signs, Direction signs, Information signs, Road markings and Vehicle markings, pages 96–107).

Laws RTO 1995 Art 50 & TSR regs 8, 13, 14, 24, 25, 25A, 25B, 26 & 33

110. Flashing headlights. Only flash your headlights to let other road users know that you are there. Do not flash your headlights to convey any other message or to intimidate other road users.

111. Never assume that flashing headlights is a signal inviting you to proceed. Use your own judgement and proceed carefully.

112. The horn. Use only while your vehicle is moving and you need to warn other road users of your presence. Never sound your horn aggressively. You **MUST NOT** use your horn
- while stationary on the road
- when driving in a built-up area between the hours of 11.30pm and 7am

except when another road user poses a danger.
Law CUR reg 114

Lighting requirements
113. You **MUST**
- ensure all sidelights and rear registration plate lights are lit between sunset and sunrise
- use headlights at night
- use headlights when visibility is seriously reduced (see Rule 226).

Night (the hours of darkness) is defined as the period between half an hour after sunset and half an hour before sunrise).
Laws RVLR regs 2, 27 & 28 & RV(DRM)R reg 9

114. You **MUST NOT**
- use any lights in a way that would dazzle or cause discomfort to other road users, including pedestrians, cyclists and horse riders
- use front or rear fog lights unless visibility is seriously reduced. You **MUST** switch them off when visibility improves to avoid dazzling other road users (see Rule 226).

In stationary queues of traffic, drivers should apply the parking brake and, once the following traffic has stopped, take their foot off the footbrake to deactivate the vehicle brake lights. This will minimise glare to road users behind until the traffic moves again.
Law RVLR reg 30

115. You should also
- use dipped headlights in dull daytime weather, to ensure that you can be seen
- keep your headlights dipped when overtaking until you are level with the other vehicle and then change to main beam if necessary, unless this would dazzle oncoming road users
- slow down, and if necessary stop, if you are dazzled by oncoming headlights.

Law RVLR reg 30

116. Hazard warning lights. These may be used when your vehicle is stationary, to warn that it is temporarily obstructing traffic. Never use them as an excuse for dangerous or illegal parking. You **MUST NOT** use hazard warning lights while driving or being towed unless you are on a motorway or unrestricted dual carriageway and you need to warn drivers behind you of a hazard or obstruction ahead. Only use them for long enough to ensure that your warning has been observed.
Law RVLR reg 30

Control of the vehicle

Braking
117. In normal circumstances. The safest way to brake is to do so early and lightly. Brake more firmly as you begin to stop. Ease the pressure off just as the vehicle comes to rest to avoid a jerky stop.

118. In an emergency. Brake immediately. Try to avoid braking so harshly that you lock your wheels. Locked wheels can lead to loss of control.

119. Skids. Skidding is usually caused by the driver braking, accelerating or steering too harshly or driving too fast for the road conditions. If skidding occurs, remove the cause by releasing the brake pedal fully or easing off the accelerator. Turn the steering wheel in the direction of the skid. For example, if the rear of the vehicle skids to the right, steer immediately to the right to recover.

Rear of the car skids to the right. Driver steers to the right.

120. ABS. If your vehicle is fitted with anti-lock brakes, you should follow the advice given in the vehicle handbook. However, in the case of an emergency, apply the footbrake firmly; do not release the pressure until the vehicle has slowed to the desired speed. The ABS should ensure that steering control will be retained, but do not assume that a vehicle with ABS will stop in a shorter distance.

121. Brakes affected by water. If you have driven through deep water your brakes may be less effective. Test them at the first safe opportunity by pushing gently on the brake pedal to make sure that they work. If they are not fully effective, gently apply light pressure while driving slowly. This will help to dry them out.

122. Coasting. This term describes a vehicle travelling in neutral or with the clutch pressed down. It can reduce driver control because
- engine braking is eliminated
- vehicle speed downhill will increase quickly
- increased use of the footbrake can reduce its effectiveness
- steering response will be affected, particularly on bends and corners
- it may be more difficult to select the appropriate gear when needed.
The vehicle is also less likely to be heard by other road users.

123. The driver and the environment. You **MUST NOT** leave a parked vehicle unattended with the engine running or leave a vehicle engine running unnecessarily while that vehicle is stationary on a public road. Generally, if the vehicle is stationary and is likely to remain so for more than a couple of minutes, you should apply the parking brake and switch off the engine to reduce emissions and noise pollution. However, it is permissible to leave the engine running if the vehicle is stationary in traffic or for diagnosing faults.
Law CUR regs 113 & 123

Speed limits

124. You **MUST NOT** exceed the maximum speed limits for the road and for your vehicle (see the table opposite). The presence of street lights generally means that there is a 30mph (48km/h) speed limit unless otherwise specified.
Laws RTRO Arts 36, 39 & 43 & MV(SL)R

125. The speed limit is the absolute maximum and does not mean it is safe to drive at that speed irrespective of conditions. Driving at speeds too fast for the road and traffic conditions is dangerous. You should always reduce your speed when
- the road layout or condition presents hazards, such as bends
- sharing the road with pedestrians, cyclists and horse riders, particularly children and motorcyclists
- weather conditions make it safer to do so
- driving at night as it is more difficult to see other road users.

Speed limits

Type of vehicle	Built-up areas* mph (km/h)	Single carriageways mph (km/h)	Dual carriageways mph (km/h)	Motorways mph (km/h)
Cars & motorcycles (including car-derived vans up to 2 tonnes maximum laden weight)	30 (48)	60 (96)	70 (112)	70 (112)
Cars towing caravans or trailers (including car-derived vans and motorcycles)	30 (48)	50 (80)	60 (96)	60 (96)
Buses, coaches and minibuses (not exceeding 12 metres (39 feet) in overall length)	30 (48)	50 (80)	60 (96)	70 (112)
Goods vehicles (not exceeding 7.5 tonnes maximum laden weight)	30 (48)	50 (80)	60 (96)	70† (112)
Goods vehicles (exceeding 7.5 tonnes maximum laden weight)	30 (48)	40 (64)	50 (80)	60 (96)

* The 30mph (48km/h) limit usually applies to all traffic on all roads with street lighting unless signs show otherwise.
† 60mph (96km/h) if articulated or towing a trailer.

126. Stopping distances. Drive at a speed that will allow you to stop well within the distance you can see to be clear. You should

- leave enough space between you and the vehicle in front so that you can pull up safely if it suddenly slows down or stops. The safe rule is never to get closer than the overall stopping distance (see Typical stopping distances diagram, opposite)
- allow at least a two-second gap between you and the vehicle in front on roads carrying faster-moving traffic and in tunnels where visibility is reduced. The gap should be at least doubled on wet roads and increased still further on icy roads
- remember, large vehicles and motorcycles need a greater distance to stop. If driving a large vehicle in a tunnel, you should allow a four-second gap between you and the vehicle in front.

If you have to stop in a tunnel, leave at least a 5-metre (16-feet) gap between you and the vehicle in front.

Use a fixed point to help measure a two-second gap

Typical stopping distances

The distances below are a general guide. The distance will depend on your attention (thinking distance), the road surface, the weather and the condition of your vehicle at the time.

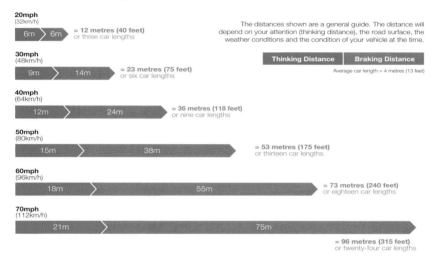

20mph (32km/h)
6m | 6m = 12 metres (40 feet) or three car lengths

30mph (48km/h)
9m | 14m = 23 metres (75 feet) or six car lengths

40mph (64km/h)
12m | 24m = 36 metres (118 feet) or nine car lengths

50mph (80km/h)
15m | 38m = 53 metres (175 feet) or thirteen car lengths

60mph (96km/h)
18m | 55m = 73 metres (240 feet) or eighteen car lengths

70mph (112km/h)
21m | 75m = 96 metres (315 feet) or twenty-four car lengths

The distances shown are a general guide. The distance will depend on your attention (thinking distance), the road surface, the weather conditions and the condition of your vehicle at the time.

Thinking Distance	Braking Distance

Average car length = 4 metres (13 feet)

Lines and lane markings on the road

Diagrams of all lines are shown in Road markings, pages 104–106.

127. A broken white line. This marks the centre of the road. When this line lengthens and the gaps shorten, it means that there is a hazard ahead. Do not cross it unless you can see the road is clear and wish to overtake or turn off.

128. Double white lines where the line nearest to you is broken. This means you may cross the lines to overtake if it is safe, provided you can complete the manoeuvre before reaching a solid white line on your side. White direction arrows on the road indicate that you need to get back onto your side of the road.

129. Double white lines where the line nearest you is solid. This means you **MUST NOT** cross or straddle it unless it is safe and you need to enter adjoining premises or a side road. You may cross the line if necessary, provided the road is clear, to pass a stationary vehicle, or overtake a pedal cycle, horse or road maintenance vehicle, if they are travelling at 10mph (16km/h) or less.

Laws RTO 1995 Art 50 & TSR reg 25

130. Areas of white diagonal stripes or chevrons painted on the road. These are to separate traffic lanes or to protect traffic turning right.
- If the area is bordered by a broken white line, you should not enter the area unless it is necessary and you can see that it is safe to do so.
- If the area is marked with chevrons and bordered by solid white lines, you **MUST NOT** enter it except in an emergency.

Laws RTO 1995 Art 50, TSR reg 8

131. Lane dividers. These are short, broken white lines which are used on wide carriageways to divide them into lanes. You should keep between them.

132. Reflective road studs may be used with white lines.
- White studs mark the lanes or the middle of the road.
- Red studs mark the left edge of the road.
- Amber studs mark the central reservation of a dual carriageway or motorway.
- Green studs mark the edge of the main carriageway at lay-bys and slip roads.
- Green/yellow studs indicate temporary adjustments to lane layouts, e.g. where roadworks are taking place.

Reflective road studs mark the lanes and edges of the carriageway

Multi-lane carriageways

Lane discipline

133. If you need to change lane, first use your mirrors and if necessary take a quick sideways glance to make sure you will not force another road user to change course or speed. When it is safe to do so, signal to indicate your intentions to other road users and when clear move over.

134. You should follow the signs and road markings and get into the lane as directed. In congested road conditions do not change lanes unnecessarily. Merging in turn is recommended but only if safe and appropriate when vehicles are travelling at a very low speed, e.g. when approaching roadworks or a road traffic incident. It is not recommended at high speed.

Single carriageway

135. Where a single carriageway has three lanes and the road markings or signs do not give priority to traffic in either direction

- use the middle lane only for overtaking or turning right. Remember, you have no more right to use the middle lane than a driver coming from the opposite direction
- do not use the right-hand lane.

136. Where a single carriageway has four or more lanes, use only the lanes that signs or markings indicate.

Dual carriageways

A dual carriageway is a road which has a central reservation to separate the carriageways.

137. On a two-lane dual carriageway you should stay in the left-hand lane. Use the right-hand lane for overtaking or turning right. After overtaking, move back to the left-hand lane when it is safe to do so.

138. On a three-lane dual carriageway, you may use the middle lane or the right-hand lane to overtake but return to the middle and then the left-hand lane when it is safe.

139. Climbing and crawler lanes. These are provided on some hills. Use this lane if you are driving a slow-moving vehicle or if there are vehicles behind you wishing to overtake. Be aware of the signs and road markings which indicate the lane is about to end.

140. Cycle lanes. These are shown by road markings and signs. You **MUST NOT** drive or park in a cycle lane marked by a solid white line during its times of operation. Do not drive or park in a cycle lane marked by a broken white line unless it is unavoidable. You **MUST NOT** park in any cycle lane whilst waiting restrictions apply.

Law RTRO Art 4(5)

141. Bus lanes. These are shown by road markings and signs that indicate which (if any) other vehicles are permitted to use the bus lane, and the times of operation. Unless otherwise indicated, you **MUST NOT** drive or ride in a bus lane during its period of operation.

Law RTRO Art 4(1, 2 & 3)

142. High-occupancy vehicle lanes (Great Britain only) and other designated vehicle lanes. Lanes may be restricted for use by particular types of vehicle; these restrictions may apply some or all of the time. The operating times and vehicle types will be indicated on the accompanying traffic signs. You **MUST NOT** drive in such lanes during their times of operation unless signs indicate that your vehicle is permitted (see Information signs, pages 102–103).

Vehicles permitted to use designated lanes may or may not include cycles, buses, taxis, licensed private hire vehicles, motorcycles, heavy goods vehicles (HGVs) and high-occupancy vehicles (HOVs). Where HOV lanes are in operation, they **MUST** only be used by

- vehicles containing at least the minimum number of people indicated on the traffic signs
- any other vehicles, such as buses and motorcycles, as indicated on signs prior to the start of the lane, irrespective of the number of occupants.

Law RTRO Art 4(5)

143. One-way streets. Traffic **MUST** travel in the direction indicated by signs. Buses and/or cycles may have a contraflow lane. Choose the correct lane for your exit as soon as you can. Do not change lanes suddenly. Unless road signs or markings indicate otherwise, you should use

- the left-hand lane when going left
- the right-hand lane when going right
- the most appropriate lane when going straight ahead.

Remember – traffic could be passing on both sides.

Laws RTO 1995 Art 50, RTRO Arts 4(5) & 5(9)

The Highway Code

General advice

144. You **MUST NOT**
- drive dangerously
- drive without due care and attention
- drive without reasonable consideration for other road users.

Law RTO 1995 Arts 10 & 12

145. You **MUST NOT** drive on or over a footway or footpath except to gain lawful access to property, or in the case of an emergency.

Law RTRO Art 3

146. Adapt your driving to the appropriate type and condition of road you are on. In particular
- do not treat speed limits as a target. It is often not appropriate or safe to drive at the maximum speed limit
- take the road and traffic conditions into account. Be prepared for unexpected or difficult situations, for example, the road being blocked beyond a blind bend. Be prepared to adjust your speed as a precaution
- where there are junctions, be prepared for road users emerging
- in side roads and country lanes look out for unmarked junctions where nobody has priority
- be prepared to stop at traffic control systems, roadworks, pedestrian crossings or traffic lights as necessary
- try to anticipate what pedestrians and cyclists might do. If pedestrians, particularly children, are looking the other way, they may step out into the road without seeing you.

147. Be considerate. Be careful of and considerate towards all types of road users, especially those requiring extra care (see Rule 204). You should
- try to be understanding if other road users cause problems; they may be inexperienced or not know the area well
- be patient; remember that anyone can make a mistake
- not allow yourself to become agitated or involved if someone is behaving badly on the road. This will only make the situation worse. Pull over, calm down and, when you feel relaxed, continue your journey
- slow down and hold back if a road user pulls out into your path at a junction. Allow them to get clear. Do not over-react by driving too close behind to intimidate them
- do not throw anything out of a vehicle, for example, cigarette ends, cans, paper or carrier bags. This can endanger other road users, particularly motorcyclists and cyclists.

148. Safe driving and riding needs concentration. Avoid distractions when driving or riding such as
- loud music (this may mask other sounds)
- trying to read maps
- inserting a cassette or CD or tuning a radio
- arguing with your passengers or other road users
- eating and drinking
- smoking.

You **MUST NOT** smoke in public transport vehicles or in vehicles used for work purposes in certain prescribed circumstances.
Law SO & SF(EVPDA)R reg 12(1)

Mobile phones and in-vehicle technology

149. You **MUST** exercise proper control of your vehicle at all times. You **MUST NOT** use a hand-held mobile phone, or similar device, when driving or when supervising a learner driver, except to call 999 or 112 in a genuine emergency when it is unsafe or impractical to stop. Never use a hand-held microphone when driving. Using hands-free equipment is also likely to distract your attention from the road. It is far safer not to use any telephone while you are driving or riding – find a safe place to stop first or use the voicemail facility and listen to messages later.
Laws RTO 1995 Arts 10, 12 & 56A & CUR regs 120 & 125A

150. There is a danger of driver distraction being caused by in-vehicle systems such as satellite navigation systems, congestion warning systems, PCs, multimedia, etc. You **MUST** exercise proper control of your vehicle at all times. Do not rely on driver assistance programs such as cruise control or lane departure warnings. They are available to assist but you should not reduce your concentration levels. Do not be distracted by maps or screen-based information (such as navigation or vehicle management systems) while driving or riding. If necessary find a safe place to stop.
Laws RTO 1995 Arts 10 & 12 & CUR reg 120

151. In slow-moving traffic. You should
- reduce the distance between you and the vehicle ahead to maintain traffic flow
- never get so close to the vehicle in front that you cannot stop safely
- leave enough space to be able to manoeuvre if the vehicle in front breaks down or an emergency vehicle needs to get past
- not change lanes to the left to overtake
- allow access into and from side roads, as blocking these will add to congestion
- be aware of cyclists and motorcyclists who may be passing on either side.

Do not block access to a side road

Driving in built-up areas

152. Residential streets. You should drive slowly and carefully on streets where there are likely to be pedestrians, cyclists and parked vehicles. In some areas a 20mph (32km/h) maximum speed limit may be in force. Look out for

- vehicles emerging from junctions or driveways
- vehicles moving off
- vehicle doors opening
- pedestrians
- children running out from between parked vehicles
- cyclists and motorcyclists.

153. Traffic-calming measures. On some roads there are features such as road humps, chicanes and narrowings which are intended to slow you down. When you approach these features reduce your speed. Allow cyclists and motorcyclists room to pass through them. Maintain a reduced speed along the whole of the stretch of road within the calming measures. Give way to oncoming road users if directed to do so by signs. You should not overtake other moving road users while in these areas.

Chicanes may be used to slow traffic down

Country roads

154. Take extra care on country roads and reduce your speed at approaches to bends, which can be sharper than they appear, and at junctions and turnings, which may be partially hidden. Be prepared for pedestrians, horse riders, cyclists, slow-moving farm vehicles or mud on the road surface. Make sure you can stop within the distance you can see to be clear. You should also reduce your speed where country roads enter villages.

155. Single-track roads. These are only wide enough for one vehicle. They may have special passing places. If you see a vehicle coming towards you, or the driver behind wants to overtake, pull into a passing place on your left, or wait opposite a passing place on your right. Give way to road users coming uphill whenever you can. If necessary, reverse until you reach a passing place to let the other road user pass. Slow down when passing pedestrians, cyclists and horse riders.

156. Do not park in passing places.

Vehicles prohibited from using roads, footways and footpaths

157. Certain motorised vehicles do not meet the construction and technical requirements for road vehicles and are generally not intended, not suitable and not legal for road, footway, footpath or cycle path use. These include most types of miniature motorcycles, also called mini motos, and motorised scooters, also called gopeds, which are powered by electric or internal combustion engines. These types of vehicle **MUST NOT** be used on roads, footways or footpaths.
Law RTO 1995 Arts 48, 56, 58, 63 & 72

158. Certain models of motorcycles, motor tricycles and quadricycles, also called quad bikes, are suitable only for off-road use and do not meet the legal standards for use on roads. Vehicles that do not meet these standards **MUST NOT** be used on roads. They **MUST NOT** be used on footways, footpaths or cycle paths either. You **MUST** make sure that any motorcycle, motor tricycle, quadricycle or any other motor vehicle meets legal standards and is properly registered, taxed and insured before using it on the roads. Even when registered, taxed and insured for the road, vehicles **MUST NOT** be used on footways or footpaths.
Laws RTO 1995 Arts 48, 56, 63 & 72 & VERA sects 1, 29, 31A & 43A

Using the road

General rules

159. Before moving off you should

- use all mirrors to check the road is clear
- look round to check the blind spots (the areas you are unable to see in the mirrors)
- signal if necessary before moving out
- look round for a final check.

Move off only when it is safe to do so.

Check the blind spot before moving off

160. Once moving you should

- keep to the left, unless road signs or markings indicate otherwise. The exceptions are when you want to overtake, turn right or pass parked vehicles or pedestrians in the road
- keep well to the left on right-hand bends. This will improve your view of the road and help avoid the risk of colliding with traffic approaching from the opposite direction
- drive with both hands on the wheel where possible. This will help you to remain in full control of the vehicle at all times
- be aware of other vehicles, especially cycles and motorcycles that may be filtering through traffic. These are more difficult to see than larger vehicles and their riders are particularly vulnerable. Give them plenty of room, especially if you are driving a long vehicle or towing a trailer
- select a lower gear before you reach a long downhill slope. This will help to control your speed
- when towing, remember the extra length will affect overtaking and manoeuvring. The extra weight will also affect the braking and acceleration.

161. Mirrors. All mirrors should be used effectively throughout your journey. You should
- use your mirrors frequently so that you always know what is behind and to each side of you
- use them in good time before you signal or change direction or speed
- be aware that mirrors do not cover all areas and there will be blind spots. You will need to look round and check.

Remember: Mirrors – Signal – Manoeuvre

Overtaking

162. Before overtaking you should make sure
- the road is sufficiently clear ahead
- road users are not beginning to overtake you
- there is a suitable gap in front of the road user you plan to overtake.

163. Overtake only when it is safe and legal to do so. You should
- not get too close to the vehicle you intend to overtake
- use your mirrors, signal when it is safe to do so, take a quick sideways glance if necessary into the blind spot area and then start to move out
- not assume that you can simply follow a vehicle ahead which is overtaking; there may only be enough room for one vehicle
- move quickly past the vehicle you are overtaking, once you have started to overtake. Allow plenty of room. Move back to the left as soon as you can but do not cut in
- take extra care at night and in poor visibility when it is harder to judge speed and distance
- give way to oncoming vehicles before passing parked vehicles or other obstructions on your side of the road
- only overtake on the left if the vehicle in front is signalling to turn right, and there is room to do so
- stay in your lane if traffic is moving slowly in queues. If the queue on your right is moving more slowly than you are, you may pass on the left
- give motorcyclists, cyclists and horse riders at least as much room as you would when overtaking a car (see Rules 211–215).

Remember: Mirrors – Signal – Manoeuvre

Give vulnerable road users at least as much space as you would a car

164. Large vehicles. Overtaking these is more difficult. You should
- drop back. This will increase your ability to see ahead and should allow the drivers of large vehicles to see you in their mirrors. Getting too close to large vehicles, including agricultural vehicles such as a tractor with a trailer or other fixed equipment, will obscure your view of the road ahead and there may be another slow-moving vehicle in front
- make sure that you have enough room to complete your overtaking manoeuvre before committing yourself. It takes longer to pass a large vehicle. If in doubt, do not overtake
- not assume you can follow a vehicle ahead which is overtaking a long vehicle. If a problem develops, they may abort overtaking and pull back in.

Do not cut in too quickly

165. You **MUST NOT** overtake
- if you would have to cross or straddle double white lines with a solid line nearest to you (but see Rule129)
- if you would have to enter an area designed to divide traffic, if it is surrounded by a solid white line
- the nearest vehicle to a signal-controlled crossing facility, especially when it has stopped to let pedestrians, equestrian traffic or cyclists to cross
- if you would have to enter a lane reserved for buses, trams or cycles during its hours of operation
- after a 'No Overtaking' sign and until you pass a sign cancelling the restriction.

Laws RTO 1995 Art 50, TSR regs 8, 25 & 25B, RTRO Art 59(4) & PCR reg 20

166. DO NOT overtake if there is any doubt, or where you cannot see far enough ahead to be sure it is safe. For example, when you are approaching
- a corner or bend
- a humpback bridge
- the brow of a hill.

167. DO NOT overtake where you might come into conflict with other road users. For example
- approaching or at a road junction on either side of the road
- where the road narrows
- when approaching a school crossing patrol
- between the kerb and a bus or tram when it is at a stop
- where traffic is queuing at junctions or roadworks
- when you would force another road user to swerve or slow down
- at a level crossing
- when a road user is indicating right, even if you believe the signal should have been cancelled. Do not take a risk; wait for the signal to be cancelled
- stay behind if you are following a cyclist approaching a roundabout or junction, and you intend to turn left
- when a tram is standing at a kerbside tram stop and there is no clearly marked passing lane for other traffic.

168. Being overtaken. If a driver is trying to overtake you, maintain a steady course and speed, slowing down if necessary to let the vehicle pass. Never obstruct drivers who wish to pass. Speeding up or driving unpredictably while someone is overtaking you is dangerous. Drop back to maintain a two-second gap if someone overtakes and pulls into the gap in front of you.

169. Do not hold up a long queue of traffic, especially if you are driving a large or slow-moving vehicle. Check your mirrors frequently, and if necessary, pull in where it is safe and let traffic pass.

Road junctions

170. Take extra care at junctions. You should
- watch out for cyclists, motorcyclists, powered wheelchairs/mobility scooters and pedestrians as they are not always easy to see. Be aware that they may not have seen or heard you if you are approaching from behind
- watch out for pedestrians crossing a road into which you are turning. If they have started to cross they have priority, so give way
- watch out for long vehicles which may be turning at a junction ahead; they may have to use the whole width of the road to make the turn (see Rule 221)
- watch out for horse riders who may take a different line on the road from that which you would expect
- not assume, when waiting at a junction, that a vehicle coming from the right and signalling left will actually turn. Wait and make sure
- look all around before emerging. Do not cross or join a road until there is a gap large enough for you to do so safely.

Give way to pedestrians who have started to cross

171. You **MUST** stop behind the line at a junction with a 'Stop' sign and a solid white line across the road. Wait for a safe gap in the traffic before you move off.

Laws RTO 1995 Art 50 & TSR regs 8 & 14

172. The approach to a junction may have a 'Give Way' sign or a triangle marked on the road. You **MUST** give way to traffic on the main road when emerging from a junction with broken white lines across the road.

Laws RTO 1995 Art 50 & TSR regs 8, 14 & 24

173. Dual carriageways. When crossing or turning right, first assess whether the central reservation is deep enough to protect the full length of your vehicle.
- If it is, then you should treat each half of the carriageway as a separate road. Wait in the central reservation until there is a safe gap in the traffic on the second half of the road.
- If the central reservation is too shallow for the length of your vehicle, wait until you can cross both carriageways in one go.

Assess your vehicle's length and do not obstruct traffic

174. Box junctions. These have criss-cross yellow lines painted on the road (see Other road markings, page 106). You **MUST NOT** enter the box until your exit road or lane is clear. However, you may enter the box and wait when you want to turn right, and are only stopped from doing so by oncoming traffic, or by other vehicles waiting to turn right. At signalled roundabouts you **MUST NOT** enter the box unless you can cross over it completely without stopping.

Laws RTO 1995 Art 50 & TSR regs 8 & 26

Enter a box junction only if your exit road is clear

Junctions controlled by traffic lights

175. You **MUST** stop behind the white 'Stop' line across your side of the road unless the light is green. If the amber light appears you may go on only if you have already crossed the stop line or are so close to it that to stop might cause a collision.

Laws RTO 1995 Art 50 & TSR regs 8 & 33

176. You **MUST NOT** move forward over the white line when the red light is showing. Only go forward when the traffic lights are green if there is room for you to clear the junction safely or you are taking up a position to turn right. If the traffic lights are not working, treat the situation as you would an unmarked junction and proceed with great care.

Laws RTO 1995 Art 50 & TSR regs 8 & 33

177. Green filter arrow. This indicates a filter lane only. Do not enter that lane unless you want to go in the direction of the arrow. You may proceed in the direction of the green arrow when it, or the full green light, shows. Give other traffic, especially cyclists, time and room to move into the correct lane.

178. Advanced stop lines. Some signal-controlled junctions have advanced stop lines to allow cycles to be positioned ahead of other traffic. Motorists, including motorcyclists, **MUST** stop at the first white line reached, and should avoid blocking the way or encroaching on the marked area at other times, e.g. if the junction ahead is blocked. If your vehicle has proceeded over the first white line at the time that the signal goes red, you **MUST** stop at the second white line, even if your vehicle is in the marked area. Allow cyclists time and space to move off when the green signal shows.

Laws RTO 1995 Art 50(1) & TSR reg 33(6)

Do not unnecessarily encroach on the cyclists' waiting area

Turning right

179. Well before you turn right you should
- use your mirrors to make sure you know the position and movement of traffic behind you
- give a right-turn signal
- take up a position just left of the middle of the road or in the space marked for traffic turning right
- leave room for other vehicles to pass on the left, if possible.

180. Wait until there is a safe gap between you and any oncoming vehicle. Watch out for cyclists, motorcyclists, pedestrians and other road users. Check your mirrors and blind spot again to make sure you are not being overtaken, then make the turn. Do not cut the corner. Take great care when turning into a main road; you will need to watch for traffic in both directions and wait for a safe gap.

Remember: Mirrors – Signal – Manoeuvre

Position your vehicle correctly to avoid obstructing traffic

181. When turning right at a crossroads where an oncoming vehicle is also turning right, there is a choice of two methods
- turn right side to right side; keep the other vehicle on your right and turn behind it. This is generally the safer method as you have a clear view of any approaching traffic when completing your turn
- left side to left side, turning in front of each other. This can block your view of oncoming vehicles, so take extra care. Cyclists and motorcyclists in particular may be hidden from your view.

Road layout, markings or how the other vehicle is positioned can determine which course should be taken.

Left – Turning right side to right side
Right – Turning left side to left side

Turning left

182. Use your mirrors and give a left-turn signal well before you turn left. Do not overtake just as you turn left and watch out for traffic coming up on your left before you make the turn, especially if driving a large vehicle. Cyclists and motorcyclists in particular may be hidden from your view.

Do not cut in on cyclists

183. When turning
- keep as close to the left as is safe and practicable
- give way to any vehicles using a bus lane, cycle lane or tramway from either direction.

Roundabouts

184. On approaching a roundabout take notice and act on all the information available to you, including traffic signs, traffic lights and lane markings which direct you into the correct lane. You should
- use **Mirrors – Signal – Manoeuvre** at all stages
- decide as early as possible which exit you need to take
- give an appropriate signal (see Rule 186). Time your signals so as not to confuse other road users
- get into the correct lane
- adjust your speed and position to fit in with traffic conditions
- be aware of the speed and position of all the road users around you.

185. When reaching the roundabout you should
- give priority to traffic approaching from your right, unless directed otherwise by signs, road markings or traffic lights
- check whether road markings allow you to enter the roundabout without giving way. If so, proceed, but still look to the right before joining

- watch out for all other road users already on the roundabout; be aware they may not be signalling correctly or at all
- look forward before moving off to make sure traffic in front has moved off.

Follow the correct procedure at roundabouts

186. Signals and position. When taking the first exit, unless signs or markings indicate otherwise
- signal left and approach in the left-hand lane
- keep to the left on the roundabout and continue signalling left to leave.

When taking an exit to the right or going full circle, unless signs or markings indicate otherwise
- signal right and approach in the right-hand lane
- keep to the right on the roundabout until you need to change lanes to exit the roundabout
- signal left after you have passed the exit before the one you want.

When taking any intermediate exit, unless signs or markings indicate otherwise
- select the appropriate lane on approach to the roundabout
- you should not normally need to signal on approach
- stay in this lane until you need to alter course to exit the roundabout
- signal left after you have passed the exit before the one you want.

When there are more than three lanes at the entrance to a roundabout, use the most appropriate lane on approach and through it.

For more specific advice on procedures at roundabouts, see Appendix on pages 126–129.

187. In all cases watch out for and give plenty of room to
- pedestrians who may be crossing the approach and exit roads
- traffic crossing in front of you on the roundabout, especially vehicles intending to leave by the next exit
- traffic which may be straddling lanes or positioned incorrectly
- motorcyclists
- cyclists and horse riders who may stay in the left-hand lane and signal right if they intend to continue round the roundabout. Allow them to do so
- long vehicles (including those towing trailers). These might have to take a different course or straddle lanes either approaching or on the roundabout because of their length. Watch out for their signals.

188. Mini-roundabouts. Approach these in the same way as normal roundabouts. All vehicles **MUST** pass round the central markings except large vehicles which are physically incapable of doing so. Remember, there is less space to manoeuvre and less time to signal. Avoid making U-turns at mini-roundabouts. Beware of others doing this.
Laws RTO 1995 Art 50 & TSR regs 8 & 14

189. At double mini-roundabouts treat each roundabout separately and give way to traffic from the right.

190. Multiple roundabouts. At some complex junctions, there may be a series of mini-roundabouts at each intersection. Treat each mini-roundabout separately and follow the normal rules.

Treat each roundabout separately

Pedestrian crossings

191. You **MUST NOT** park on a crossing or in the area covered by the zig-zag lines. You **MUST NOT** overtake the moving vehicle nearest the crossing or the vehicle nearest the crossing which has stopped to give way to pedestrians.
Laws RTRO Art 59(4) & PCR regs 16, 18 & 20

192. In queuing traffic, you should keep the crossing clear.

Keep the crossing clear

193. You should take extra care where the view of either side of the crossing is blocked by queuing traffic or incorrectly parked vehicles. Pedestrians may be crossing between stationary vehicles.

194. Allow pedestrians plenty of time to cross and do not harass them by revving your engine or edging forward.

195. Zebra crossings. As you approach a zebra crossing
- look out for pedestrians waiting to cross and be ready to slow down or stop to let them cross
- you **MUST** give way when a pedestrian has moved onto a crossing
- allow more time for stopping on wet or icy roads
- do not wave or use your horn to invite pedestrians across; this could be dangerous if another vehicle is approaching
- be aware of pedestrians approaching from the side of the crossing.
A zebra crossing with a central island is two separate crossings (see Rule 20).
Laws RTRO Art 59(4) & PCR reg 21

Signal-controlled crossings

196. Pelican crossings. These are signal-controlled crossings where flashing amber follows the red 'Stop' light. You **MUST** stop when the red light shows. When the amber light is flashing, you **MUST** give way to any pedestrians on the crossing. If the amber light is flashing and there are no pedestrians on the crossing, you may proceed with caution.
Laws RTRO Art 59(4) & PCR regs 10, 19 & 22

Allow pedestrians to cross when the amber light is flashing

197. Pelican crossings which go straight across the road are one crossing, even when there is a central island. You **MUST** wait for pedestrians who are crossing from the other side of the island.
Laws RTRO Art 59(4) & PCR reg 22

198. Give way to anyone still crossing after the signal for vehicles has changed to green. This advice applies to all crossings.

199. Toucan, puffin and equestrian crossings. These are similar to pelican crossings, but there is no flashing amber phase; the light sequence for traffic at these three crossings is the same as at traffic lights. If the signal-controlled crossing is not working, proceed with extreme caution.

Reversing

200. Choose an appropriate place to manoeuvre. If you need to turn your vehicle around, wait until you find a safe place. Try not to reverse or turn round in a busy road; find a quiet side road or drive round a block of side streets.

201. Do not reverse from a side road into a main road. When using a driveway, reverse in and drive out if you can.

202. Look carefully before you start reversing. You should
- use all your mirrors
- check the 'blind spot' behind you (the part of the road you cannot see easily in the mirrors)
- check there are no pedestrians (particularly children), cyclists, other road users or obstructions in the road behind you.

Reverse slowly while
- checking all around
- looking mainly through the rear window
- being aware that the front of your vehicle will swing out as you turn.

Get someone to guide you if you cannot see clearly.

Check all round when reversing

203. You **MUST NOT** reverse your vehicle farther than necessary.
Law CUR reg 122

Road users requiring extra care

204. The most vulnerable road users are pedestrians, cyclists, motorcyclists and horse riders. It is particularly important to be aware of children, elderly and disabled people, and learner and inexperienced drivers and riders.

Pedestrians

205. There is a risk of pedestrians, especially children, stepping unexpectedly into the road. You should drive with the safety of children in mind at a speed suitable for the conditions.

206. Drive carefully and slowly when
- in crowded shopping streets, Home Zones and Quiet Lanes (see Rule 218) or residential areas
- driving past bus and tram stops; pedestrians may emerge suddenly into the road
- passing parked vehicles, especially ice cream vans; children are more interested in ice cream than traffic and may run into the road unexpectedly
- needing to cross a footway, footpath, cycle lane or cycle track; for example, to reach or leave a driveway. Give way to pedestrians on the footway or footpath and to cyclists on the cycle lane or cycle track
- reversing into a side road; look all around the vehicle and give way to any pedestrians who are already crossing the road into which you are turning
- the footway or footpath is closed due to street repairs and pedestrians are directed to use the road
- approaching pedestrians on narrow rural roads without a footway or footpath. Always slow down and be prepared to stop if necessary, giving them plenty of room as you drive past.

Watch out for children in busy areas

207. Particularly vulnerable pedestrians. These include

- children and older pedestrians who may not be able to judge your speed and could step into the road in front of you. At 40mph (64km/h) your vehicle will probably kill any pedestrian it hits. At 20mph (32km/h) there is only a 1 in 20 chance of the pedestrian being killed. So kill your speed
- older pedestrians who may need more time to cross the road. Be patient and allow them to cross in their own time. Do not hurry them by revving your engine or edging forward
- people with disabilities. People with hearing impairments may not be aware of your vehicle approaching. Those with walking difficulties require more time
- blind or partially sighted people, who may be carrying a white cane or using a guide dog. They may not be able to see you approaching
- deafblind people who may be carrying a white cane with a red band or using a dog with a red and white harness. They may not see or hear instructions or signals.

208. Near schools. Drive slowly and be particularly aware of young cyclists and pedestrians. In some places, there may be a flashing amber signal below the 'School' or 'Patrol' warning sign which tells you that there may be children crossing the road ahead. Drive very slowly until you are clear of the area.

209. Drive carefully when passing a stationary bus carrying school children or showing 'School Bus' markings or signs (see Vehicle markings, page 107) as children may be getting on or off.

210. You **MUST** stop when a school crossing patrol shows a 'stop for children' sign (see Signals by authorised persons and Signs giving orders, pages 95 and 96).
Law RTRO Art 60

Motorcyclists and cyclists

211. It is often difficult to see motorcyclists and cyclists, especially when they are coming up from behind, coming out of junctions, at roundabouts, overtaking you or filtering through traffic. Always look out for them before you emerge from a junction; they could be approaching faster than you think. When turning right across a line of slow-moving or stationary traffic, look out for cyclists or motorcyclists on the inside of the traffic you are crossing. Be especially careful when turning, and when changing direction or lane. Be sure to check mirrors and blind spots carefully.

Look out for motorcyclists and cyclists at junctions

212. When passing motorcyclists and cyclists, give them plenty of room (see Rules162–167). If they look over their shoulder it could mean that they intend to pull out, turn right or change direction. Give them time and space to do so.

213. Motorcyclists and cyclists may suddenly need to avoid uneven road surfaces and obstacles such as drain covers or oily, wet or icy patches on the road. Give them plenty of room and pay particular attention to any sudden change of direction they may have to make.

Other road users

214. Animals. When passing animals, drive slowly. Give them plenty of room and be ready to stop. Do not scare animals by sounding your horn, revving your engine or accelerating rapidly once you have passed them. Look out for animals being led, driven or ridden on the road and take extra care. Keep your speed down at bends and on narrow country roads. If a road is blocked by a herd of animals, stop and switch off your engine until they have left the road. Watch out for animals on unfenced roads.

215. Horse riders and horse-drawn vehicles. Be particularly careful of horse riders and horse-drawn vehicles, especially when overtaking. Always pass wide and slowly. Horse rides are often children, so take extra care and remember riders may ride in double file when escorting a young or inexperienced horse or rider. Look out for horse riders' and horse drivers' signals and heed a request to slow down or stop. Take great care and treat all horses as a potential hazard; they can be unpredictable, despite the efforts of their rider/driver.

216. Older drivers. Their reactions may be slower than other drivers. Make allowance for this.

217. Learners and inexperienced drivers. They may not be so skilful at anticipating and responding to events. Be particularly patient with learner drivers, restricted drivers and young drivers. Drivers are required to display R plates for one year after passing their test, not counting any periods of disqualification or revocation (see Annexe 8 – Safety Code for New Drivers, pages 122–123).

218. Home Zones and Quiet Lanes (Great Britain only). These are places where people could be using the whole of the road for a range of activities such as children playing or for a community event. You should drive slowly and carefully and be prepared to stop or allow people extra time to make space for you to pass them in safety.

Other vehicles

219. Emergency and Incident Support vehicles. You should look and listen for ambulances, fire engines, police, doctors or other emergency vehicles using blue, red or green lights and sirens or flashing headlights or for Driver and Vehicle Agency Enforcement Officer vehicles using flashing amber lights. When one approaches do not panic. Consider the route of such a vehicle and take appropriate action to let it pass, while complying with all traffic signs. If necessary, pull to the side of the road and stop, but try to avoid stopping before the brow of a hill, a bend or narrow section of road. Do not endanger yourself or other road users and avoid mounting the kerb. Do not brake harshly on approach to a junction or roundabout, as a following vehicle may not have the same view as you.

220. Powered vehicles used by disabled people. These small vehicles travel at a maximum speed of 8mph (12km/h). On a dual carriageway where the speed limit exceeds 50mph (80km/h) they **MUST** have a flashing amber beacon, but on other roads you may not have that advance warning (see Rules 36–46 inclusive).

Law RVLR regs 20(1) & 29

221. Large vehicles. These may need extra road space to turn or to deal with a hazard that you are not able to see. If you are following a large vehicle, such as a bus or articulated lorry, be aware that the driver may not be able to see you in the mirrors. Be prepared to stop and wait if it needs room or time to turn.

Large vehicles need extra room

222. Large vehicles can block your view. Your ability to see and to plan ahead will be improved if you pull back to increase your separation distance. Be patient, as larger vehicles are subject to lower speed limits than cars and motorcycles. Many large vehicles may be fitted with speed limiting devices which will restrict speed to 56mph (90km/h) even on a motorway.

223. Buses, coaches and trams. Give priority to these vehicles when you can do so safely, especially when they signal to pull away from stops. Look out for people getting off a bus or tram and crossing the road.

224. Electric vehicles. Be careful of electric vehicles such as milk floats and trams. Trams move quickly but silently and cannot steer to avoid you.

225. Vehicles with flashing amber beacons. These warn of a slow-moving or stationary vehicle (such as a Driver and Vehicle Agency vehicle, salt spreader, snow plough or recovery vehicle) or abnormal loads, so approach with caution. On restricted dual carriageways, motor vehicles first used on or after 1 January 1947 with a maximum speed of 25mph (40km/h) or less (such as tractors) **MUST** use a flashing amber beacon. (Also see Rule 220.)
Law RVLR reg 20

Driving in adverse weather conditions

226. You **MUST** use headlights when visibility is seriously reduced, generally when you cannot see for more than 100 metres (328 feet). You may also use front or rear fog lights but you **MUST** switch them off when visibility improves (see Rule 236).
Law RVLR regs 28 & 30

227. Wet weather. In wet weather, stopping distances will be at least double those required for stopping on dry roads (see Rule 126). This is because your tyres have less grip on the road. In wet weather

- you should keep well back from the vehicle in front. This will increase your ability to see and plan ahead
- if the steering becomes unresponsive, it probably means that water is preventing the tyres from gripping the road. Ease off the accelerator and slow down gradually
- the rain and spray from vehicles may make it difficult to see and be seen
- be aware of the dangers of spilt diesel that will make the surface very slippery (see Annexe 6, pages 118–120)
- take extra care around pedestrians, cyclists, motorcyclists and horse riders.

Icy and snowy weather

228. In winter check the local weather forecast for warnings of icy or snowy weather. **DO NOT** drive in these conditions unless your journey is essential. If it is, take great care and allow more time for your journey. Take an emergency kit of de-icer and ice scraper, torch, warm clothing and boots, first aid kit, jump leads and a shovel, together with a warm drink and emergency food in case you get stuck or your vehicle breaks down.

229. Before you set off

- you **MUST** be able to see, so clear all snow and ice from all your windows
- you **MUST** ensure that lights are clean and number plates are clearly visible and legible
- make sure the mirrors are clear and the windows are demisted thoroughly
- remove all snow that might fall off into the path of other road users
- check your planned route is clear of delays and that no further snowfalls or severe weather are predicted.

Laws CUR reg 35, RVLR reg 26 & VERA sect 43 & RV(DRM) reg 11

Make sure your windscreen is completely clear

230. When driving in icy or snowy weather
- drive with care, even if the roads have been treated
- keep well back from the road user in front as stopping distances can be ten times greater than on dry roads
- take care when overtaking vehicles spreading salt or other de-icer, particularly if you are riding a motorcycle or cycle
- watch out for snowploughs which may throw out snow on either side. Do not overtake them unless the lane you intend to use has been cleared
- be prepared for the road conditions to change over relatively short distances
- listen to travel bulletins and take note of variable message signs that may provide information about weather, road and traffic conditions ahead.

231. Drive extremely carefully when the roads are icy. Avoid sudden distractions as these could cause loss of control. You should
- drive at a slow speed in as high a gear as possible; accelerate and brake very gently
- drive particularly slowly on bends where loss of control is more likely. Brake progressively on the straight before you reach a bend. Having slowed down, steer smoothly round the bend, avoiding sudden actions
- check your grip on the road surface when there is snow or ice by choosing a safe place to brake gently. If the steering feels unresponsive this may indicate ice and your vehicle losing its grip on the road. When travelling on ice, tyres make virtually no noise.

Windy weather

232. High-sided vehicles are most affected by windy weather, but strong gusts can also blow a car, cyclist, motorcyclist or horse rider off course. This can happen on open stretches of road exposed to strong crosswinds, or when passing bridges or gaps in hedges.

233. In very windy weather your vehicle may be affected by turbulence created by large vehicles. Motorcyclists are particularly affected, so keep well back from them when they are overtaking a high-sided vehicle.

Fog

234. Before entering fog check your mirrors then slow down. If the word 'Fog' is shown on a roadside signal or overhead gantry but the road is clear, be prepared for a bank of fog or drifting patchy fog ahead. Even if it seems to be clearing, you can suddenly find yourself in thick fog.

235. When driving in fog you should
- use your lights as required (see Rule 226)
- keep a safe distance behind the vehicle in front. Rear lights can give a false sense of security
- be able to pull up well within the distance you can see clearly. This is particularly important on motorways and dual carriageways, as vehicles are travelling faster
- use your windscreen wipers and demisters
- beware of other drivers not using headlights
- not accelerate to get away from a vehicle which is too close behind you
- check your mirrors before you slow down. Then use your brakes so that your brake lights warn drivers behind you that you are slowing down
- stop in the correct position at a junction with limited visibility and listen for traffic. When you are sure it is safe to emerge, do so positively and do not hesitate in a position that puts you directly in the path of approaching vehicles.

236. You **MUST NOT** use front or rear fog lights unless visibility is seriously reduced (see Rule 226) as they dazzle other road users and can obscure your brake lights. You **MUST** switch them off when visibility improves.
Law RVLR regs 28 & 30

Hot weather

237. Keep your vehicle well ventilated to avoid drowsiness. Be aware that the road surface may become soft or if it rains after a dry spell it may become slippery. These conditions could affect your steering and braking. If you are dazzled by bright sunlight, slow down and if necessary, stop.

Waiting and parking

238. You **MUST NOT** wait or park on yellow lines during the times of operation shown on nearby time plates (or zone entry signs if in a Controlled Parking Zone) – see Information signs and Road markings, pages 102 and 105. Double yellow lines indicate a prohibition of waiting at any time even if there are no upright signs. You **MUST NOT** wait or park, or stop to set down and pick up passengers, on school entrance markings (see Road markings, page 106) when upright signs indicate a prohibition of stopping.

Laws RTRO Art 4(5) & R(RW)O

Parking

239. Use off-street parking areas, or bays marked out with white lines on the road as parking places, wherever possible. If you have to stop on the roadside

- do not park facing against the traffic flow
- stop as close as you can to the side
- do not stop too close to a vehicle displaying a Blue Badge: remember, the occupant may need more room to get in or out
- you **MUST** switch off the engine, headlights and fog lights
- you **MUST** apply the handbrake before leaving the vehicle
- you **MUST** ensure you do not hit anyone when you open your door. Check for cyclists or other traffic
- it is safer for your passengers (especially children) to get out of the vehicle on the side next to the kerb
- lock your vehicle.

Laws CUR regs 113, 121 & 123, RVLR reg 30, RTO 1995 Art 58 & R(RW)O

Check before opening your door

240. You **MUST NOT** stop or park on
- the carriageway or the hard shoulder of a motorway except in an emergency (see Rule 270)
- a pedestrian crossing, including the area marked by the zig-zag lines (see Rule 191)
- within 15 metres (50 feet) of any junction, except in a lay-by in specified circumstances or in a designated parking area (see Traffic signs, page 97)
- a clearway (see Traffic signs, page 97)
- taxi bays as indicated by upright signs and markings
- an urban clearway within its hours of operation, even when a broken white line is on your side of the road, except to pick up or set down passengers (see Traffic signs, page 97)
- a road marked with double white lines, except to pick up or set down passengers or to load or unload where this is not prohibited
- a bus stop marked on the carriageway or bus stop lay-bys unless otherwise indicated by signs
- a bus, tram or cycle lane during its period of operation
- a cycle track.

Laws RTO 1995 Art 32, RTRO Art 4(5), TSO Art 25, CUR reg 119 & R(RW)O

241. You **MUST NOT** park in parking spaces reserved for specific users, such as Blue Badge holders, residents or motorcycles, unless entitled to do so.
Laws RTRO Arts 14(1) & 19(1) & CSDPA sect 14B

242. You **MUST NOT** leave your vehicle or trailer in a dangerous position or where it causes any unnecessary obstruction of the road.
Laws RTO 1995 Art 32, RO Art 88 & CUR reg 119

243. DO NOT stop or park
- near a school entrance
- anywhere you would prevent access for Emergency Services
- at or near a bus stop or taxi rank
- on the approach to a level crossing/tramway crossing
- near the brow of a hill or humpback bridge
- opposite a traffic island or (if this would cause an obstruction) another parked vehicle
- where you would force other traffic to enter a tram lane
- where the kerb has been lowered to help wheelchair users and powered mobility vehicles
- in front of an entrance to a property

- on a bend
- where you would obstruct cyclists' use of cycle facilities

except when forced to do so by stationary traffic.

244. DO NOT park partially or wholly on the footway or footpath unless signs permit it. Parking on the footway or footpath can obstruct and seriously inconvenience pedestrians, people in wheelchairs or with visual impairments and people with prams or pushchairs.

245. Controlled Parking Zones. The zone entry signs indicate the times when the waiting restrictions within the zone are in force. Parking may be allowed in some places at other times. Otherwise parking will be within separately signed and marked bays.

246. Goods vehicles. Vehicles with a maximum laden weight of over 7.5 tonnes (including any trailer) **MUST NOT** be parked on a verge, footway or footpath or any land situated between carriageways, without police permission. The only exception is when parking is essential for loading and unloading, in which case the vehicle **MUST NOT** be left unattended.

Law RTO 1995 Art 30(1)

247. Loading and unloading. Do not load or unload where there are yellow markings on the kerb and upright signs advise that restrictions are in place (see Road markings, pages 105–106). This may be permitted where parking is otherwise restricted.

Law RTRO Art 4(5)

Parking at night

248. You **MUST NOT** park on a road at night facing against the direction of the traffic flow unless in a recognised parking space.

Laws CUR reg 117 & RVLR reg 27

249. All vehicles **MUST** display parking lights when parked on a road or a lay-by on a road with a speed limit greater than 30mph (48km/h).

Law RVLR reg 27

250. Cars, goods vehicles not exceeding 1525kg unladen weight, invalid carriages, motorcycles and pedal cycles may be parked without lights on a road (or lay-by) with a speed limit of 30mph (48km/h) or less if they are

- at least 15 metres (50 feet) away from any junction, close to the kerb and facing in the direction of the traffic flow
- in a recognised parking place or lay-by.

Other vehicles and trailers, and all vehicles with projecting loads, **MUST NOT** be left on a road at night without lights.

Laws RVLR reg 27, R(RW)O & CUR reg 94(9)

251. Parking in fog. It is especially dangerous to park on the road in fog. If it is unavoidable, leave your parking lights or sidelights on.

252. Parking on hills. If you park on a hill you should

- park close to the kerb and apply the handbrake firmly
- select a forward gear and turn your steering wheel away from the kerb when facing uphill
- select reverse gear and turn your steering wheel towards the kerb when facing downhill
- use 'park' if your car has an automatic gearbox.

Turn your wheels away from the kerb when parking facing uphill

Turn your wheels towards the kerb when parking facing downhill

Decriminalised Parking Enforcement (DPE)

DPE, already in place in Northern Ireland, is becoming increasingly common throughout the United Kingdom as more authorities take on this role. The Department for Regional Development's Roads Service or the local traffic authorities in Great Britain assume responsibility for enforcing many parking contraventions in place of the police. Further details on DPE may be found at the following websites:

www.roadsni.gov.uk/parking/index.htm

www.parking-appeals.gov.uk (outside London)

www.parkingandtrafficappeals.gov.uk (inside London)

Motorways

Many other Rules apply to motorway driving, either wholly or in part: Rules 46, 57, 83–126, 130–134, 139, 144, 146–151, 160, 161, 219, 221–222, 225, 226–237, 274–278, 280, and 281–290.

General

253. Prohibited vehicles. Motorways **MUST NOT** be used by pedestrians, holders of provisional motorcycle or car licences, riders of motorcycles under 50cc, cyclists, horse riders, certain slow-moving vehicles and those carrying oversized loads (except by special permission), agricultural vehicles and powered wheelchairs/powered mobility scooters (see Rules 36–46 incl.)

Laws RO Art 16 & sch 1 & MTR reg 2

254. Traffic on motorways usually travels faster than on other roads, so you have less time to react. It is especially important to use your mirrors earlier and look much further ahead than you would on other roads.

Motorway signals

255. Motorway signals (see Motorway signals, page 92) are used to warn you of a danger ahead. For example, there may be an incident, fog, a spillage or road workers on the carriageway which you may not immediately be able to see.

256. Signals situated on the central reservation apply to all lanes. On very busy stretches, signals may be overhead with a separate signal for each lane.

257. Amber flashing lights. These warn of a hazard ahead. The signal may show a temporary maximum speed limit, lanes that are closed or a message such as 'Fog'. Adjust your speed and look out for the danger until you pass a signal which is not flashing or one that gives the 'All clear' sign and you are sure it is safe to increase your speed.

258. Red flashing lights. If red lights on the overhead signals flash above your lane and a red 'X' is showing, you **MUST NOT** go beyond the signal in that lane. If red lights flash on a signal in the central reservation or at the side of the road, you **MUST NOT** go beyond the signal in any lane.

Laws RTO 1995 Art 50 & TSR regs 8 & 33(3)

Driving on the motorway

259. Joining the motorway. When you join the motorway you will normally approach it from a road on the left (a slip road) or from an adjoining motorway. You should

- give priority to traffic already on the motorway
- check the traffic on the motorway and match your speed to fit safely into the traffic flow in the left-hand lane
- not cross solid white lines that separate lanes or use the hard shoulder
- stay on the slip road if it continues as an extra lane on the motorway
- remain in the left-hand lane long enough to adjust to the speed of traffic before considering overtaking.

On the motorway

260. When you can see well ahead and the road conditions are good, you should

- drive at a steady cruising speed which you and your vehicle can handle safely and is within the speed limit (see Rule 124)
- keep a safe distance from the vehicle in front and increase the gap on wet or icy roads, or in fog (see Rules 126 and 235).

261. You **MUST NOT** exceed 70mph (112km/h), or the maximum speed limit permitted for your vehicle (see Rule 124). If a lower speed limit is in force, either permanently or temporarily, at roadworks for example, you **MUST NOT** exceed the lower limit. On some motorways, mandatory motorway signals (which display the speed within a red ring) are used to vary the maximum speed limit to improve traffic flow. You **MUST NOT** exceed this speed limit.
Law RO Art 20, RTRO Art 39 & MV(SL)R

262. The monotony of driving on a motorway can make you feel sleepy. To minimise the risk, follow the advice in Rule 91.

263. You **MUST NOT** reverse, cross the central reservation, or drive against the traffic flow. If you have missed your exit, or have taken the wrong route, carry on to the next exit.
Laws MTR regs 4, 7 & 10

Lane discipline

264. You should always drive in the left-hand lane when the road ahead is clear. If you are overtaking a number of slower-moving vehicles, you should return to the left-hand lane as soon as you are safely past. Slow-moving or speed-restricted vehicles should always remain in the left-hand lane of the carriageway unless overtaking. You **MUST NOT**

drive on the hard shoulder except in an emergency or if directed to do so by the police or by signs.
Law MTR regs 3 & 8

265. The right-hand lane of a motorway with three or more lanes should not be used if you are driving
- any vehicle drawing a trailer
- a goods vehicle with a maximum laden weight exceeding 3.5 tonnes but not exceeding 7.5 tonnes, which is required to be fitted with a speed limiter
- a goods vehicle with a maximum laden weight exceeding 7.5 tonnes
- a passenger vehicle with a maximum laden weight exceeding 7.5 tonnes constructed or adapted to carry more than eight seated passengers in addition to the driver
- a passenger vehicle with a maximum laden weight not exceeding 7.5 tonnes which is constructed or adapted to carry more than eight seated passengers in addition to the driver, which is required to be fitted with a speed limiter.

266. Approaching a junction. Look well ahead for signals or signs. Direction signs may be placed over the road. If you need to change lanes, do so in good time. At some junctions a lane may lead directly off the motorway. Only get in that lane if you wish to go in the direction indicated on the overhead signs.

Overtaking
267. Do not overtake unless you are sure it is safe and legal to do so. Overtake only on the right. You should
- check your mirrors
- take time to judge the speeds correctly
- make sure that the lane you will be joining is sufficiently clear ahead and behind
- take a quick sideways glance into the blind spot area to verify the position of a vehicle that may have disappeared from your view in the mirror
- remember that traffic may be coming up behind you very quickly. Check all your mirrors carefully. Look out for motorcyclists. When it is safe to do so, signal in plenty of time, then move out
- ensure you do not cut in on the vehicle you have overtaken
- be especially careful at night and in poor visibility when it is harder to judge speed and distance.

268. Do not overtake on the left or move to a lane on your left to overtake. In congested conditions, where adjacent lanes of traffic are moving at similar speeds, traffic in left-hand lanes may sometimes be moving faster than traffic to the right. In these conditions you may keep up with the traffic in your lane even if this means passing traffic in the lane to your right. Do not weave in and out of lanes to overtake.

269. Hard shoulder. You **MUST NOT** use the hard shoulder for overtaking. In areas where an Active Traffic Management (ATM) scheme is in force, the hard shoulder may be used as a running lane. You will know when you can use this because a speed limit sign will be shown above all open lanes, including the hard shoulder. A red cross or blank sign above the hard shoulder means that you **MUST NOT** drive on the hard shoulder except in an emergency or breakdown. Emergency refuge areas have also been built into these areas for use in cases of emergency or breakdown.

Hard shoulder bus lanes. On some stretches of motorway, hard shoulders are used as bus lanes during specified times of the day. The operation of these bus lanes is controlled using variable message signing. In the event of an emergency or incident the bus lane reverts to being a hard shoulder. You **MUST NOT** use the bus lane for any purpose other than an emergency or breakdown.
Law MTR regs 3 & 8

Overhead gantry showing red cross over hard shoulder

Stopping
270. You **MUST NOT** stop on the carriageway, hard shoulder, slip road, central reservation or verge except in an emergency, or when told to do so by the police, an emergency sign or by flashing red light signals. Do not stop on the hard shoulder to either make or receive mobile phone calls.
Law MTR regs 5, 8 & 10

271. You **MUST NOT** pick up or set down anyone, or walk on a motorway, except in an emergency.
Laws RO Art 20 & MTR reg 13

Leaving the motorway
272. Unless signs indicate that a lane leads directly off the motorway, you will normally leave the motorway by a slip road on your left. You should
- watch out for the signs letting you know you are getting near your exit
- move into the left-hand lane well before reaching your exit
- signal left in good time and reduce your speed on the slip road as necessary.

273. On leaving the motorway or using a link road between motorways, your speed may be higher than you realise – 50mph (80km/h) may feel like 30mph (48km/h). Check your speedometer and adjust your speed accordingly. Some slip roads and link roads have sharp bends, so you will need to slow down.

Breakdowns and incidents

Breakdowns
274. If your vehicle breaks down, think first of all other road users and
- get your vehicle off the road if possible
- warn other traffic by using your hazard warning lights if your vehicle is causing an obstruction
- help other road users see you by wearing light-coloured or fluorescent clothing in daylight and reflective clothing at night or in poor visibility
- put a warning triangle on the road at least 45 metres (147 feet) behind your broken-down vehicle on the same side of the road, or use other permitted warning devices if you have them. Always take great care when placing or retrieving them, but never use them on motorways
- keep your sidelights on if it is dark or visibility is poor
- do not stand (or let anybody else stand) between your vehicle and oncoming traffic
- at night or in poor visibility do not stand where you will prevent other road users seeing your lights.

Additional rules for the motorway

275. If your vehicle develops a problem, leave the motorway at the next exit or pull into a service area. If you cannot do so, you should

- pull onto the hard shoulder and stop as far to the left as possible, with your wheels turned to the left
- try to stop near an emergency telephone (situated at approximately 1-mile [1.6km] intervals along the hard shoulder)
- leave the vehicle by the left-hand door and ensure your passengers do the same. You **MUST** leave any animals in the vehicle or, in an emergency, keep them under proper control on the verge. Never attempt to place a warning triangle on a motorway
- do not put yourself in danger by attempting even simple repairs
- ensure that passengers keep away from the carriageway and hard shoulder, and that children are kept under control
- walk to an emergency telephone on your side of the carriageway (follow the arrows on the posts at the back of the hard shoulder) – the telephone is free of charge and connects directly to the police. Use these in preference to a mobile phone (see Rule 283). Always face the traffic when you speak on the phone
- give full details to the police; also inform them if you are a vulnerable motorist such as disabled, older or travelling alone
- return and wait near your vehicle (well away from the carriageway and hard shoulder)
- if you feel at risk from another person, return to your vehicle by a left-hand door and lock all doors. Leave your vehicle again as soon as you feel this danger has passed.

Laws MTR regs 12 & 13

Keep well back from the hard shoulder

276. Before you rejoin the carriageway after a breakdown, build up speed on the hard shoulder and watch for a safe gap in the traffic. Be aware that other vehicles may be stationary on the hard shoulder.

277. If you cannot get your vehicle onto the hard shoulder
- do not attempt to place any warning device on the carriageway
- switch on your hazard warning lights
- leave your vehicle only when you can safely get clear of the carriageway.

278. Disabled drivers. If you have a disability which prevents you from following the above advice you should
- stay in your vehicle
- switch on your hazard warning lights
- display a 'Help' pennant or, if you have a car or mobile telephone, contact the emergency services and be prepared to advise them of your location.

Obstructions

279. If anything falls from your vehicle (or any other vehicle) onto the road, stop and retrieve it only if it is safe to do so.

280. Motorways. On a motorway do not try to remove the obstruction yourself. Stop at the next emergency telephone and call the police.

Incidents

281. Warning signs or flashing lights. If you see or hear emergency or incident support vehicles in the distance, be aware there may be an incident ahead (see Rule 219). Police officers and Roads Service officials may be required to work in the carriageway, for example dealing with debris, collisions or conducting rolling road blocks. Police officers will use rear-facing flashing red and blue lights in these situations. Watch out for such signals, slow down and be prepared to stop. You **MUST** follow any directions given by police officers as to whether you can safely pass the incident or blockage.

Laws RTO 1995 Art 49 & RTO 1981 Art 180

282. When passing the scene of an incident or crash do not be distracted or slow down unnecessarily (for example if an incident is on the other side of a dual carriageway). This may cause a collision or traffic congestion, but see Rule 283.

283. If you are involved in a collision or stop to give assistance
- use your hazard warning lights to warn other traffic
- ask drivers to switch off their engines and stop smoking
- arrange for the emergency services to be called immediately with full details of the incident location and any casualties (on a motorway, use the emergency telephone which allows easy location by the emergency services. If you use a mobile phone, first make sure you have identified your location from the marker posts on the side of the hard shoulder)
- move uninjured people away from the vehicles to safety; on a motorway this should, if possible, be well away from the traffic, the hard shoulder and the central reservation
- do not move injured people from their vehicles unless they are in immediate danger from fire or explosion
- do not remove a motorcyclist's helmet unless it is essential to do so
- be prepared to give first aid as shown in Annexe 7, First aid on the road, pages 121–122
- stay at the scene until emergency services arrive.

If you are involved in any other medical emergency on the motorway you should contact the emergency services in the same way.

Incidents involving dangerous goods

284. Vehicles carrying dangerous goods in packages will be marked with plain orange reflective plates. Road tankers and vehicles carrying tank containers of dangerous goods will have hazard warning plates (see Vehicle markings, page 107).

285. If an incident involves a vehicle containing dangerous goods, follow the advice in Rule 283 and, in particular
- switch off engines and **DO NOT SMOKE**
- keep well away from the vehicle and do not be tempted to try to rescue casualties as you yourself could become one
- call the emergency services and give as much information as possible about the labels and markings on the vehicle. **DO NOT** use a mobile phone close to a vehicle carrying inflammable loads.

Documentation

286. If you are involved in a collision which causes damage or injury to any other person, vehicle, animal or property, you **MUST**
- stop
- give your own and the vehicle owner's name and address, and the registration number of the vehicle, to anyone having reasonable grounds for requiring them
- if you do not give your name and address at the time of the collision, report the collision to the police immediately.

Law RTO 1981 Arts 175 & 176

287. If another person is injured and you do not produce your insurance certificate at the time of the collision to a police officer or to anyone having reasonable grounds to request it, you **MUST**

- report the collision to the police immediately
- produce your insurance certificate for the police as soon as reasonably practicable.

Law RTO 1981 Art 175

Roadworks

288. When the 'Road Works Ahead' sign is displayed, you will need to be more watchful and look for additional signs providing more specific instructions. Observe all signs – they are there for your safety and the safety of road workers.

- You **MUST NOT** exceed any temporary maximum speed limit.
- Use your mirrors and get into the correct lane for your vehicle in good time and as signs direct.
- Do not switch lanes to overtake queuing traffic.
- Take extra care near cyclists and motorcyclists as they are vulnerable to skidding on grit, mud or other debris at roadworks.
- Where lanes are restricted due to roadworks, merge in turn (see Rule 134).
- Do not drive through an area marked off by traffic cones.
- Watch out for traffic entering or leaving the works area, but do not be distracted by what is going on there. Concentrate on the road ahead, not the roadworks.
- Bear in mind that the road ahead may be obstructed by the works or by slow-moving or stationary traffic.
- Keep a safe distance – there could be queues in front.

To obtain further information about roadworks see Other information, page 125.

Law RTRO Art 43

Additional rules for high-speed roads

289. Take special care on motorways and other high-speed dual carriageways.

- One or more lanes may be closed to traffic and a lower speed limit may apply.
- Works vehicles that are slow moving or stationary with a large 'Keep Left' or 'Keep Right' sign on the back are sometimes used to close lanes for repairs, and a flashing light arrow may also be used to make the works vehicle more conspicuous from a distance and give earlier warning to drivers that they need to move over to the next lane.

- Check mirrors, slow down and change lanes if necessary.
- Keep a safe distance from the vehicle in front (see Rule 126).

290. Contraflow systems mean that you may be travelling in a narrower lane than normal and with no permanent barrier between you and oncoming traffic. The hard shoulder may be used for traffic, but be aware that there may be broken-down vehicles ahead of you. Keep a good distance from the vehicle ahead and observe any temporary speed limits.

Level crossings

291. A level crossing is where a road crosses a railway or tramway line. Approach and cross it with care. Never drive onto a crossing until the road is clear on the other side and do not get too close to the car in front. Never stop or park on, or near a crossing.

292. Overhead electric lines. It is dangerous to touch overhead electric lines. You **MUST** obey the safe height warning road signs and you should not continue forward onto the railway if your vehicle touches any height barrier or bells. The clearance available is usually 5 metres (16 feet 6 inches) but may be lower.
Laws RTO 1995 Art 50(1) & TSR reg 15(2)

293. Controlled Crossings. Most crossings have traffic light signals with a steady amber light, twin flashing red stop lights (see Light signals controlling traffic page 92 and Warning signs, pages 98–99) and an audible alarm for pedestrians. They may have full, half or no barriers.
- You **MUST** always obey the flashing red stop lights.
- You **MUST** stop behind the white line across the road.
- Keep going if you have already crossed the white line when the amber light comes on.
- Do not reverse onto or over a controlled crossing.
- You **MUST** wait if a train goes by and the red lights continue to flash. This means another train will be passing soon.
- Only cross when the lights go off and barriers open.
- Never zig-zag around half-barriers, they lower automatically because a train is approaching.
- At crossings where there are no barriers, a train is approaching when the lights show.

Laws RTO 1995 Art 50 & TSR regs 8 & 33

Stop when the traffic lights show

294. Railway telephones. If you are driving a large or slow-moving vehicle, a long, low vehicle with a risk of grounding, or herding animals, a train could arrive before you are clear of the crossing. You **MUST** obey any sign instructing you to use the railway telephone to obtain permission to cross. You **MUST** also telephone when clear of the crossing if requested to do so.
Laws RTO 1995 Art 50 & TSR regs 8 & 14

295. Crossings without traffic lights. Vehicles should stop and wait at the barrier or gate when it begins to close and not cross until the barrier or gate opens.

296. User-operated gates or barriers. Some crossings have 'Stop' signs and small red and green lights. You **MUST NOT** cross when the red light is showing, only cross if the green light is on. If crossing with a vehicle, you should
• open the gates or barriers on both sides of the crossing
• check that the green light is still on and cross quickly
• close the gates or barriers when you are clear of the crossing.
Laws RTO 1995 Art 50 & TSR reg 8

297. If there are no lights, follow the procedure in Rule 296. Stop, look both ways and listen before you cross. If there is a railway telephone, always use it to contact the signal operator to make sure it is safe to cross. Inform the signal operator again when you are clear of the crossing.

298. Open crossings. These have no gates, barriers, attendant or traffic lights but will have a 'Give Way' sign. You should look both ways, listen and make sure there is no train coming before you cross.

299. Incidents and breakdowns. If your vehicle breaks down, or if you have a collision on a crossing you should

- get everyone out of the vehicle and clear of the crossing immediately
- use a railway telephone if available to tell the signal operator. Follow the instructions you are given
- move the vehicle clear of the crossing if there is time before a train arrives. If the alarm sounds, or the amber light comes on, leave the vehicle and get clear of the crossing immediately.

Tramways

Currently applies to Great Britain only. Legislative references relate to Great Britain legislation.

300. You **MUST NOT** enter a road, lane or other route reserved for trams. Take extra care where trams run along the road. You should avoid driving directly on top of the rails and should take care where trams leave the main carriageway to enter the reserved route, to ensure you do not follow them. The width taken up by trams is often shown by tram lanes marked by white lines, yellow dots or by a different type of road surface. Diamond-shaped signs and white light signals give instructions to tram drivers only.

Law RTRA sects 5 & 8

301. Take extra care where the track crosses from one side of the road to the other and where the road narrows and the tracks come close to the kerb. Tram drivers usually have their own traffic signals and may be permitted to move when you are not. Always give way to trams. Do not try to race or overtake them or pass them on the inside, unless they are at tram stops or stopped by tram signals and there is a designated tram lane for you to pass.

302. You **MUST NOT** park your vehicle where it would get in the way of trams or where it would force other drivers to do so. Do not stop on any part of a tram track, except in a designated bay where this has been provided alongside and clear of the track. When doing so, ensure that all parts of your vehicle are outside the delineated tram path. Remember that a tram cannot steer round an obstruction.

Law RTRA sects 5 & 8

303. Tram stops. Where the tram stops at a platform, either in the middle or at the side of the road, you **MUST** follow the route shown by the road signs and markings. At stops without platforms you **MUST NOT** drive between a tram and the left-hand kerb when a tram has stopped to pick up passengers. If there is no alternative route signed, do not overtake the tram – wait until it moves off.
Law RTRA sects 5 & 8

304. Look out for pedestrians, especially children, running to catch a tram approaching a stop.

305. Always give priority to trams, especially when they signal to pull away from stops, unless it would be unsafe to do so. Remember that they may be carrying large numbers of standing passengers who could be injured if the tram had to make an emergency stop. Look out for people getting off a bus or tram and crossing the road.

306. All road users, but particularly cyclists and motorcyclists, should take extra care when driving or riding close to or crossing the tracks, especially if the rails are wet. You should take particular care when crossing the rails at shallow angles, on bends and at junctions. It is safest to cross the tracks directly at right angles. Other road users should be aware that cyclists and motorcyclists may need more space to cross the tracks safely.

307. Overhead electric lines. Tramway overhead wires are normally 5.8 metres (19 feet) above any carriageway, but can be lower. You should ensure that you have sufficient clearance between the wire and your vehicle (including any load you are carrying) before driving under an overhead wire. Drivers of vehicles with extending cranes, booms, tipping apparatus or other types of variable height equipment should ensure that the equipment is fully lowered. Where overhead wires are set lower than 5.8 metres (19 feet), these will be indicated by height clearance markings – similar to 'low bridge' signs. The height clearances on these plates should be carefully noted and observed. If you are in any doubt as to whether your vehicle will pass safely under the wires, you should always contact the local police or the tramway operator. Never take a chance as this can be extremely hazardous.

Light signals controlling traffic

Traffic light signals

RED means 'Stop'. Wait behind the stop line on the carriageway

RED AND AMBER also means 'Stop'. Do not pass through or start until GREEN shows

GREEN means you may go on if the way is clear. Take special care if you intend to turn left or right and give way to pedestrians who are crossing

AMBER means 'Stop' at the stop line. You may go on only if the AMBER appears after you have crossed the stop line or are so close to it that to pull up might cause a collision

A GREEN ARROW may be provided in addition to the full green signal if movement in a certain direction is allowed before or after the full green phase. If the way is clear you may go but only in the direction shown by the arrow. You may do this whatever other lights may be showing. White light signals may be provided for trams

Flashing red lights

Alternately flashing red lights mean YOU MUST STOP

At level crossings, lifting bridges, airfields, fire stations, etc.

Motorway signals

You **MUST NOT** proceed further in this lane

Change lane

Reduced visibility ahead

Lane ahead closed

Temporary maximum speed advised and information message

Leave motorway at next exit

Temporary maximum speed advised

End of restriction

Lane control signals

Green arrow – lane available to traffic facing the sign
Red crosses – lane closed to traffic facing the sign
White diagonal arrow – change lanes in direction shown

Signals to other road users

Direction indicator signals

I intend to move out to the right or turn right

I intend to move in to the left or turn left or stop on the left

Brake light signals

I am applying the brakes

Reversing light signals

I intend to reverse

These signals should not be used except for the purposes described.

Arm signals

For use when direction indicator signals are not used, or when necessary to reinforce direction indicator signals and stop lights. *Also for use by pedal cyclists and those in charge of horses.*

I intend to move in to the left or turn left

I intend to move out to the right or turn right

I intend to slow down or stop

Signals by authorised persons

Police officers

Stop

| Traffic approaching from the front | Traffic approaching from both front and behind | Traffic approaching from behind |

To beckon traffic on

| From the side | From the front | From behind |

Arm signals to persons controlling traffic

| I want to go straight on | I want to turn left; use either hand | I want to turn right |

Driver and Vehicle Agency

Driver and Vehicle Agency Enforcement Officer

These officers have powers to stop/direct vehicles and will be using hand signals and light signals similar to those used by police. You **MUST** obey any signals given (see Rule 107).

School crossing patrols

Not ready to cross children

Barrier to stop children crossing

Ready to cross children, vehicles must be prepared to stop

All vehicles must stop

Traffic signs

Signs giving orders

Signs with red circles are mostly prohibitive.
Plates below signs qualify their message.

Entry to
20 mph zone

End of
20 mph zone

Maximum
speed

National speed
limit applies

School crossing
patrol

Stop and
give way

Give way to
traffic on
major road

Manually operated temporary
STOP and GO signs

No entry for
vehicular traffic

No vehicles
except bicycles
being pushed

No cycling

No motor
vehicles

No buses
(over 8
passenger
seats)

No
overtaking

No
towed
caravans

No vehicles
carrying
explosives

No vehicle or
combination of
vehicles over
length shown

No vehicles
over
height shown

No vehicles
over
width shown

Give priority to
vehicles from
opposite
direction

No right turn

No left turn

No
U-turns

No goods vehicles
over maximum
gross weight
shown (in tonnes)
except for loading
and unloading

Note: Although *The Highway Code* shows many of the signs commonly in use, a
comprehensive explanation of our signing system is given in the booklet *Know Your
Traffic Signs*, which is on sale at booksellers. The booklet also illustrates and explains
the vast majority of signs the road user is likely to encounter. The signs illustrated in
The Highway Code are not all drawn to the same scale.

WEAK BRIDGE

No vehicles over maximum gross weight shown (in tonnes)

Parking restricted to permit holders

No stopping during period indicated except for buses

No stopping during times shown except for as long as necessary to set down or pick up passengers

No waiting

No stopping (Clearway)

Signs with blue circles but no red border mostly give positive instruction.

Ahead only

Turn left ahead (right if symbol reversed)

Turn left (right if symbol reversed)

Keep left (right if symbol reversed)

Vehicles may pass either side to reach same destination

Mini-roundabout (roundabout circulation – give way to vehicles from the immediate right)

Route to be used by pedal cycles only

Segregated pedal cycle and pedestrian route

Minimum speed

End of minimum speed

Buses and cycles only

Trams only

Pedestrian crossing point over tramway

One-way traffic (note: compare circular 'Ahead only' sign)

With-flow bus and cycle lane

Contraflow bus lane

With-flow pedal cycle lane

Warning signs

Mostly triangular

Distance to
'STOP' line
ahead

Dual
carriageway
ends

Road narrows on
right (left if
symbol reversed)

Road
narrows on
both sides

Distance to
'Give Way'
line ahead

Crossroads

Junction on
bend ahead

T-junction with
priority over
vehicles from
the right

Staggered
junction

Traffic merging
from left ahead

The priority through route is indicated by the broader line.

Double bend first
to left (symbol
may be reversed)

Bend to right
(or left if symbol
reversed)

Roundabout

Uneven road

Plate below
some signs

Two-way
traffic crosses
one-way road

Two-way traffic
straight ahead

Opening or
swing bridge
ahead

Low-flying aircraft
or sudden
aircraft noise

Falling or
fallen rocks

Traffic signals
not in use

Traffic signals

Slippery road

Steep hill
downwards

Steep hill
upwards

Gradients may be shown as a ratio i.e. 20% = 1:5

Tunnel ahead

Trams
crossing
ahead

Level crossing
with barrier or
gate ahead

Level crossing
without barrier
or gate ahead

Level crossing
without barrier

Warning signs – continued

Patrol

School crossing
patrol ahead
(some signs
have amber
lights which flash
when crossings
are in use)

Frail (or blind or
disabled if shown)
pedestrians likely to
cross road ahead

**No footway
for 400 yds**

Pedestrians
in road ahead

Zebra
crossing

**Safe height
16'-6"**

Overhead electric
cable; plate
indicates
maximum height
of vehicles which
can pass safely

Available width of
headroom indicated

Sharp deviation of route
to left (or right if
chevrons reversed)

Light signals
ahead at level
crossing, airfield
or bridge

Miniature warning lights
at level crossings

Cattle

Wild animals

Wild horses
or ponies

Accompanied
horses or
ponies

Cycle route
ahead

Ice

Risk of ice

**Queues
likely**

Traffic queues
likely ahead

**Humps for
½ mile**

Distance over
which road
humps extend

Hidden dip

Other danger;
plate indicates
nature of
danger

**Soft verges
for 2 miles**

Soft verges

Side winds

Hump bridge

Ford

Worded warning
sign

Quayside or
river bank

Risk of
grounding

Direction signs

Mostly rectangular

Signs on motorways – blue backgrounds

At a junction leading directly
into a motorway (junction number
may be shown
on a black background)

On approaches to
junctions (junction number
on black background)

Route confirmatory
sign after junction

Downward pointing arrows mean 'Get in lane'
The left-hand lane leads to a different destination from the other lanes.

The panel with the inclined arrow indicates the destinations which can be reached
by leaving the motorway at the next junction

Signs on primary routes - green backgrounds

On approaches to junctions

On approaches to junctions

At the junction

Route confirmatory sign after junction

On approach to a junction

Blue panels indicate that the motorway starts at the junction ahead.
Motorways shown in brackets can also be reached along the route indicated.
White panels indicate local or non-primary routes leading from the junction ahead.
Brown panels show the route to tourist attractions.
The name of the junction may be shown at the top of the sign.
The aircraft symbol indicates the route to an airport.
A symbol may be included to warn of a hazard or restriction along that route.

Green background signs – continued

Primary route forming part of a ring road

Signs on non-primary and local routes - black borders

On approaches to junctions

At the junction

Direction to toilets with access for the disabled

Green panels indicate that the primary route starts at the junction ahead.
Route numbers on a blue background show the direction to a motorway.
Route numbers on a green background show the direction to a primary route.

Other direction signs

Picnic site

National Trust Property

Direction to a car park

Tourist attraction

Direction to camping and caravan site

Advisory route for lorries

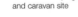

Route for pedal cycles forming part of a network

Recommended route for pedal cycles to place shown

Route for pedestrians

Symbols showing emergency diversion route for motorway and other main road traffic

Diversion route

Information signs

All rectangular

Entrance to controlled parking zone

Entrance to congestion charging zone

End of controlled parking zone

Advance warning of restriction or prohibition ahead

Parking place for solo motorcycles

With-flow bus lane ahead which pedal cycles, motorcycles and taxis may also use

Lane designated for use by high occupancy vehicles (HOV) - see rule 142

Vehicles permitted to use an HOV lane ahead

End of motorway

Start of motorway and point from which motorway regulations apply

Appropriate traffic lanes at junction ahead

Traffic on the main carriageway coming from right has priority over joining traffic

Additional traffic joining from left ahead. Traffic on main carriageway has priority over joining traffic from right hand lane of slip road

Traffic in right hand lane of slip road joining the main carriageway has prority over left hand lane

'Countdown' markers at exit from motorway (each bar represents 100 yards to the exit). Green-backed markers may be used on primary routes and white-backed markers with black bars on other routes. At approaches to concealed level crossings white-backed markers with red bars may be used. Although these will be erected at equal distances the bars do not represent 100 yard intervals.

Motorway service area sign

Information signs – continued

Priority over oncoming vehicles

Traffic has priority over oncoming vehicles

Hospital ahead with Accident and Emergency facilities

Tourist information point

No through road for vehicles

Recommended route for pedal cycles

Home Zone Entry

Area in which cameras are used to enforce traffic regulations

Bus lane on road at junction ahead

Roadworks signs

Road works

Loose chippings

Temporary hazard at roadworks

Temporary lane closure (the number and position of arrows and red bars may be varied according to lanes open and closed)

Slow-moving or stationary works vehicle blocking a traffic lane. Pass in the direction shown by the arrow.

Mandatory speed limit ahead

Road works 1 mile ahead

End of road works and any temporary restrictions, including speed limits

Signs used on the back of slow-moving or stationary vehicles warning of a lane closed ahead by a works vehicle. There are no cones on the road.

Lane restrictions at roadworks ahead

One lane crossover at contraflow roadworks

Road markings

Across the carriageway

Stop line at signals or police control

Stop line at 'Stop' sign

Stop line for pedestrians at a level crossing

Give way to traffic on major road (can also be used at mini roundabouts)

Give way to traffic from the right at a roundabout

Give way to traffic from the right at a mini-roundabout

Along the carriageway

Edge line

Centre line
See Rule 127

Hazard warning line
See Rule 127

Double white lines
See Rules 128 and 129

See Rule 130

Lane line See Rule 131

Along the edge of the carriageway

Waiting restrictions

Waiting restrictions indicated by yellow lines apply to the carriageway, footway or footpath. You may stop to load or unload (unless there are also loading restrictions as described below) or while passengers board or alight. Double yellow lines mean no waiting at any time, unless there are signs that specifically indicate seasonal restrictions. The times at which the restrictions apply for other road markings are shown on nearby plates or on entry signs to controlled parking zones. If no days are shown on the signs, the restrictions are in force every day including Sundays and bank holidays. White bay markings and upright signs (see below) indicate where parking is allowed.

| No waiting at any time | No waiting during times shown on sign | Waiting is limited to the duration specified during the days and times shown |

Red Route stopping controls

Red lines are used on some roads instead of yellow lines. In London the double and single red lines used on Red Routes indicate that stopping to park, load/unload or to board and alight from a vehicle (except for a licensed taxi or if you hold a Blue Badge) is prohibited. The red lines apply to the carriageway, pavement and verge. The times that the red line prohibitions apply are shown on nearby signs, but the double red line ALWAYS means no stopping at any time. On Red Routes you may stop to park, load/unload in specially marked boxes and adjacent signs specify the times and purposes and duration allowed. A box MARKED IN RED indicates that it may only be available for the purpose specified for part of the day (e.g. between busy peak periods). A box MARKED IN WHITE means that it is available throughout the day.

RED AND SINGLE YELLOW LINES CAN ONLY GIVE A GUIDE TO THE RESTRICTIONS AND CONTROLS IN FORCE AND SIGNS, NEARBY OR AT A ZONE ENTRY, MUST BE CONSULTED.

| No stopping at any time | No stopping during times shown on sign | Parking is limited to the duration specified during the days and times shown | Only loading may take place at the times shown for up to a maximum duration of 20 mins |

On the kerb or at the edge of the carriageway

Loading restrictions on roads other than Red Routes

Yellow marks on the kerb or at the edge of the carriageway indicate that loading or unloading is prohibited at the times shown on the nearby black and white plates. You may stop while passengers board or alight. If no days are indicated on the signs the restrictions are in force every day including Sundays and Bank Holidays.

ALWAYS CHECK THE TIMES SHOWN ON THE PLATES.

Lengths of road reserved for vehicles loading and unloading are indicated by a white 'bay' marking with the words 'Loading Only' and a sign with the white on blue 'trolley' symbol. This sign also shows whether loading and unloading is restricted to goods vehicles and the times at which the bay can be used. If no times or days are shown it may be used at any time. Vehicles may not park here if they are not loading or unloading.

No loading or unloading at any time

No loading or unloading at the times shown

Loading bay

Other road markings

Keep entrance clear of stationary vehicles, even if picking up or setting down children

Warning of 'Give Way' just ahead

Parking space reserved for vehicles named

See Rules 240 & 243

See Rule 141

Box junction - See Rule 174

Do not block that part of the carriageway indicated

Indication of traffic lanes

Vehicle markings

Large goods vehicle rear markings

Motor vehicles over 7500 kilograms maximum gross weight and trailers over 3500 kilograms maximum gross weight

The vertical markings are also required to be fitted to builders' skips placed in the road, commercial vehicles or combinations longer than 13 metres (optional on combinations between 11 and 13 metres)

Hazard warning plates

Certain tank vehicles carrying dangerous goods must display hazard information panels

The panel illustrated is for flammable liquid. Diamond symbols indicating other risks include:

The above panel will be displayed by vehicles carrying certain dangerous goods in packages

Projection markers

Both required when load or equipment (eg crane jib) overhangs front or rear by more than two metres

Other

School bus (displayed in front or rear window of bus or coach)

The Highway Code

Annexes

1. You and your bicycle

Make sure that you feel confident of your ability to ride safely on the road. Be sure that
- you choose the right size and type of cycle for comfort and safety
- lights and reflectors are kept clean and in good working order
- tyres are in good condition and inflated to the pressure shown on the tyre
- gears are working correctly
- the chain is properly adjusted and oiled
- the saddle and handlebars are adjusted to the correct height.

You **MUST**
- ensure your brakes are efficient
- ensure a working bell or horn is fitted
- at night, use lit front and rear lights and have a red rear reflector.

Laws RV(T)R reg 7 & RVLR reg 21

Cycle training can help both children and adults, especially those adults returning to cycling to develop the skills needed to cycle safely on today's roads.

All cyclists should consider the benefits of undertaking cycle training. For information, contact your local Department of the Environment Road Safety Education Office.

2. Motorcycle licence requirements

If you have a provisional motorcycle licence or a full car licence you may ride motorcycles up to 125cc and 11kW power output, with L plates on public roads. To obtain your full motorcycle licence you **MUST** pass a motorcycle Theory Test and then a Practical Test.

If you have a full moped licence and wish to obtain full motorcycle entitlement, you will be required to take a motorcycle theory test if you did not take a separate theory test when you obtained your moped licence. You **MUST** then pass a practical motorcycle test.

Law MV(DL)R reg 31(1)

Light motorcycle licence (A1): you take a test on a motorcycle of between 75 and 125cc. If you pass you may ride a motorcycle up to 125cc with power output up to 11kW.

Standard motorcycle licence (A): if your test vehicle is between 120 and 125cc and capable of more than 62mph (100km/h) you will be given a standard (A) licence. You will then be restricted to motorcycles of up to 25kW for two years, not counting any periods of disqualification or revocation. After two years you may ride any size of machine.

You **MUST NOT** carry a pillion passenger or pull a trailer until you have passed your test.

Law MV(DL)R reg 12

Moped licence requirements

A moped **MUST** have an engine capacity not exceeding 50cc, not weigh more than 250kg and be designed to have a maximum speed not exceeding 31mph (50km/h). From June 2003 all EC Type Approved mopeds have been restricted to 28mph (45km/h).

Law RTO 1981 (as amended) Art 19D

To ride a moped, learners **MUST**
- be 16 or over
- have a provisional moped licence.

You **MUST** first pass the theory test for motorcycles and then the moped practical test to obtain your full moped licence.

If you have a full car licence or motorcycle licence you are qualified to ride a moped without L plates.

Note. For motorcycle and moped riders wishing to upgrade, the following give exemption from taking the motorcycle theory test
- full A1 motorcycle licence gained on or after 1 January 1997
- full moped licence, if gained on or after 1 July 1996.

Law MV(DL)R regs 27(3), 31 & 32

3. Motor vehicle documentation, learner and restricted driver requirements

Documents

Driving licence. You **MUST** have a valid signed driving licence for the category of vehicle you are driving. You **MUST** inform the Driver and Vehicle Agency (DVA) if you change your name and/or address.
Law RTO 1981 Art 3

Holders of non-European Community licences who are now resident in the UK may only drive on that licence for a maximum of 12 months from the date they become resident in this country. To ensure continuous driving entitlement
- a UK provisional licence should be obtained and a driving test(s) passed before the 12-month period elapses, or
- in the case of a driver who holds a licence from a country which has been designated in law for licence exchange purposes, the driver should exchange the licence for a UK one.

MOT. Cars and motorcycles **MUST** normally pass an MOT test (vehicle test) four years from the date of the first registration and every year after that. You **MUST NOT** drive a motor vehicle without displaying a vehicle test certificate, when it should have one. Exceptionally, you may drive to a pre-arranged test appointment or to a garage for repairs required for the test. Driving an unroadworthy motor vehicle may invalidate your insurance.
Law RTO 1995 Arts 61, 63, 63A, 65 & 69

Insurance. To use a motor vehicle on the road, you **MUST** have a valid insurance policy. This **MUST** at least cover you for injury or damage to a third party while using that motor vehicle. Before driving any motor vehicle, make sure that it has this cover for your use or that your own insurance provides adequate cover. You **MUST NOT** drive a motor vehicle without insurance. Also, be aware that even if a road traffic collision is not your fault, you may still be held liable by insurance companies.
Law RTO 1981 Art 90

Uninsured drivers can now be automatically detected by roadside cameras.

The types of cover available are indicated below:

Third-Party insurance – this is often the cheapest form of insurance, and is the minimum cover required by law. It covers anyone you might injure or whose property you might damage. It does not cover damage to your own motor vehicle or injury to yourself.

Third-Party, Fire and Theft insurance – similar to third-party, but also covers you against your motor vehicle being stolen, or damaged by fire.

Comprehensive insurance – this is the most expensive but the best insurance. Apart from covering other persons and property against injury or damage, it also covers damage to your own motor vehicle, up to the market value of that vehicle, and personal injury to yourself.

Registration certificate. Registration certificates (also called harmonised registration certificates) are issued for all motor vehicles used on the road, describing them (make, model, etc.) and giving details of the registered keeper. You **MUST** notify the Driver and Vehicle Agency in Coleraine as soon as possible when you buy or sell a motor vehicle, or if you change your name or address. The buyer and seller are responsible for completing the registration certificates. The seller is responsible for forwarding them to the DVA. The procedures are explained on the back of the registration certificates.
Law RV(R&L)R Part IV

Vehicle Excise Duty (VED). All motor vehicles used or kept on public roads **MUST** display a valid Vehicle Excise Duty disc (tax disc) displayed at all times. Even motor vehicles exempt from duty **MUST** display a tax disc at all times.
Law VERA sects 29 and 33

Statutory Off-Road Notification (SORN). This is a notification to the DVA that a motor vehicle is not being used on the road. If you want to keep a motor vehicle untaxed and off the public road you **MUST** declare SORN – it is an offence not to do so. You then won't have to pay any road tax for that vehicle for a period of 12 months. You need to send a further declaration after that period if the vehicle is still off the public road. The SORN will end if you sell the vehicle and the new owner will become immediately responsible.
Law RV(R&L)R reg 26 sch 4

Production of documents. You **MUST** be able to produce your driving licence and counterpart, a valid insurance certificate and (if appropriate) a valid MOT certificate, when requested by a police officer. If you cannot do this you may be asked to take them to a police station within seven days.
Law RTO 1981 Arts 180 & 180A

Learner drivers

Learners driving a car **MUST** hold a valid provisional licence. They **MUST** be supervised by someone at least 21 years old who holds a full EC/EEA licence for that type of car (automatic or manual) and has held one for at least three years.
Laws MV(DL)R reg 12 & RTO 1981 Art 3

Vehicles. Any vehicle driven by a learner **MUST** display red L plates. Plates **MUST** conform to legal specifications and **MUST** be clearly visible to others from in front of the vehicle and from behind. Plates should be removed or covered when not being driven by a learner (except on driving school vehicles).

The speed limit for vehicles displaying L plates is 45mph (72km/h), except goods vehicles, buses and coaches on a motorway.
Laws MV(DL)R reg 12, RTO 1981 Art 19 & MV(SLRE)R reg 2

You **MUST** pass the theory test (if one is required) and then a practical driving test for the category of vehicle you wish to drive before driving unaccompanied.
Law MV(DL)R reg 30

Restricted drivers

After passing the driving test for a motor car or a motorcycle, you must display amber R plates for a period of one year from the date of passing the test. The plates **MUST** conform to legal specifications and **MUST** be clearly visible to others from in front of the vehicle and from behind. Plates should be removed or covered when not being driven by a restricted driver. The maximum permitted speed for any vehicle displaying R plates is 45mph (72km/h), whether or not the vehicle is being driven by a restricted driver.
Laws RTO 1981 Art 19A & MV(PR)R

4. The road user and the law
Road traffic law
The following list can be found abbreviated throughout the Code. It is not intended to be a comprehensive guide, but a guide to some of the important points of law. For the precise wording of the law, please refer to the various Orders and Regulations (as amended) indicated in the Code. Abbreviations are listed on the following page.

Most of the provisions apply on all roads throughout Northern Ireland. A road includes a public road, any part of a public road and any bridges or tunnels over or through which a public road passes, and any street, carriageway, highway or roadway to which the public has access (RTO 1995 Art 2).

It is important to note that references to 'road' therefore generally include footways, footpaths and cycle tracks, and many roadways and driveways on private land (including many car parks). In most cases, the law will apply to them and there may be additional rules for particular paths or ways. Some serious driving offences, including drink-driving offences, also apply to all public places, for example public car parks.

Chronically Sick & Disabled Persons (NI) Act 1978   CSPDA
Criminal Justice (NI) Order 1994   CJO
Motor Vehicles (Construction & Use) Regulations (NI) 1999   CUR
Motor Vehicles (Construction & Use) (Amendment No.5)
    Regulations (NI) 2003   CU(A)R
Motor Vehicles (Constructions & Use) (Amendment)
    Regulations (NI) 2005   CU(A)R
Horses (Protective Headgear for Young Riders) (NI) Order 1990   H(PHYR)O
Horses (Protective Headgear for Young Riders)
    Regulations (NI) 1992   H(PHYR)R
Motor Cycles (Eye Protectors) Regulations (NI) 2004   MC(EP)R
Motor Cycles (Protective Headgear) Regulations (NI) 1999   MC(PH)R
Motor Vehicles (Driving Licences) Regulations (NI) 1996   MV(DL)R
Motor Vehicles Driving Licences (Amendment)
    Regulations (NI) 2003 (4 sets of Regulations)   MVDL(A)R
Motor Vehicles (Invalid Carriages) Regulations (NI) 1999   MV(IC)R
Motor Vehicles (Prescribed Restrictions) Regulations (NI) 1996   MV(PR)R
Motor Vehicles (Speed Limits) Regulations (NI) 1989   MV(SL)R
Motor Vehicles (Speed Limit Restriction) (Exemption)
    Regulations (NI) 1998   MV(SLRE)R
Motor Vehicles (Wearing of Seat Belts) Regulations (NI) 1993   MV(WSB)R
Motor Vehicles (Wearing of Seat Belts by Children in Front Seats)
    Regulations (NI) 1993 and 2007   MV(WSBCFS)R
Motor Vehicles (Wearing of Seat Belts) (Amendment)
    Regulations (NI) 2007 and 2008   MV(WSB)(A)R
Motorways Traffic Regulations (NI) 2008   MTR
Road Traffic (NI) Order 1981, 1995 or 2007 (as indicated)   RTO
Road Traffic Offenders (NI) Order 1996   RTOO
Road Traffic Regulation (NI) Order 1997   RTRO
Road Vehicles Lighting (Amendment) Regulations (NI) 2007   RVL(A)R
Road Vehicles Lighting Regulations (NI) 2000   RVLR
Road Vehicles (Registration & Licensing) Regulations 2002   RV(R&L)R
Road Traffic (New Drivers) (NI) Order 1998   RT(ND)O
Road Vehicles (Traffic) Regulations 1933   RV(T)R
Roads (NI) Order 1993   RO
Roads (Restriction of Waiting) Order (NI) 1982   R(RW)O
Road Vehicles (Display of Registration Marks) Regulations 2001   RV(DRM)R
Smoking (NI) Order 2006   SO
Smoke-Free (Exemptions, Vehicles, Penalties & Discounted
    Amounts) Regulations (NI) 2007   SF(EVPDA)R
Traffic Signs Regulations (NI) 1997   TSR
Vehicle Excise and Registration Act 1994   VERA
Zebra Pelican & Puffin Pedestrian Crossing Regulations (NI) 2006   PCR

Orders and regulations from 1988 can be viewed on the Office of Public Sector information website (www.opsi.gov.uk). Orders and regulations prior to 1988 are only available in their original print format which can be obtained from The Stationery Office.

5. Penalties

Parliament sets the maximum penalties for road traffic offences. The seriousness of the offence is reflected in the maximum penalty. It is for the courts to decide what sentence to impose according to circumstances.

The penalty table on the next page indicates some of the main offences, and the associated penalties. There is a wide range of other more specific offences which, for the sake of simplicity, are not shown here. The penalty points and disqualification system is described below.

Penalty points and disqualification

The penalty points system is intended to deter drivers and motorcyclists from following unsafe motoring practices. Certain non-motoring offences, e.g. failure to rectify vehicle defects, can also attract penalty points. The court **MUST** order points to be endorsed on the licence according to the fixed number or the range set by Parliament. The accumulation of penalty points acts as a warning to drivers that they risk disqualification if further offences are committed.

Law RTOO Arts 49 & 50

A driver or motorcyclist who accumulates 12 or more penalty points within a three-year period **MUST** be disqualified. This will be for a minimum period of six months, or longer if the driver or motorcyclist has previously been disqualified.

Law RTOO Art 40

For every offence which carries penalty points the court has a discretionary power to order the licence holder to be disqualified. This may be for any period the court thinks fit, but will usually be between a week and a few months.

In the case of serious offences, such as dangerous driving and drink-driving, the court **MUST** order disqualification. The minimum period is 12 months, but for repeat offenders or where the alcohol level is high, it may be longer. For example, a second drink-drive offence in the space of 10 years will result in a minimum of three years' disqualification.

Law RTOO Art 35

The Highway Code

Penalty Table

Offence	Maximum Penalties			
	Imprisonment	Fine	Disqualification	Penalty Points
*Causing death, or grievous bodily injury by dangerous driving	14 years	Unlimited	Obligatory – 2 years minimum	3–11 (if exceptionally not disqualified)
*Dangerous driving	5 years	Unlimited	Obligatory	3–11 (if exceptionally not disqualified)
*Causing death, or grievous bodily injury by careless driving when under the influence of drink or drugs	14 years	Unlimited	Obligatory – 2 years minimum	3–11 (if exceptionally not disqualified)
Aggravated vehicle taking causing death or grievous bodily injury	14 years	Unlimited	Obligatory	3–11
Careless and inconsiderate driving	-	£5,000	Discretionary	3–9
**Driving while unfit through drink or drugs or with excess alcohol; or failing to provide a specimen for analysis	6 months	£5,000	Obligatory	3–11 (if exceptionally not disqualified)
Failing to stop after an accident (collision) or failing to report an accident (collision)	6 months	£5,000	Discretionary	5–10
Driving when disqualified	2 years	Unlimited	Discretionary	6
Causing death or grievous bodily injury by careless or inconsiderate driving	5 years	Unlimited	Obligatory	3–11
Driving without insurance	6 months	£5,000	Discretionary	6–8
Causing death or grievous bodily injury by driving unlicensed, uninsured or while disqualified	2 years	Unlimited	Obligatory	3–11
Speeding	-	£1,000 (£2,500 for motorway offences)	Discretionary	3–6 or 3 (fixed penalty)
Traffic light offences	-	£1,000	Discretionary	3
No MOT certificate	-	£1,000	-	-
Seat belt offences	-	£500	-	3
Dangerous cycling	-	£2,500	-	-
Careless cycling	-	£1,000	-	-
Failing to identify driver of a vehicle	-	£1,000	Discretionary	6

* Where a court disqualifies a person on conviction for one of these offences, it must order an extended retest and for those offences marked
**it must order an ordinary retest. The courts also have discretion to order a retest for any other offence which carries obligatory endorsement, an extended retest where disqualification is for repeated offences and an ordinary retest in any other case.

Furthermore, in some serious cases, the court **MUST** (in addition to imposing a fixed period of disqualification) order the offender to be disqualified until they pass a driving test. In other cases the court has a discretionary power to order such disqualification. The test may be of ordinary or extended length according to the nature of the offence.
Law RTOO Art 41

New drivers. Special rules as set out below apply for a period of two years from the date of passing their first driving test, to drivers and motorcyclists from
• the UK, EU/EEA, the Isle of Man, the Channel Islands or Gibraltar who passed their first driving test in any of those countries
• other foreign countries who have to pass a UK driving test to gain a UK licence, in which case the UK driving test is treated as their first driving test; and
• other foreign countries who (without needing a test) exchanged their licence for a UK licence and subsequently passed a UK driving test to drive another type of vehicle, in which case the UK driving test is treated as their first driving test. For example a driver who exchanges a foreign licence (car) for a UK licence (car) and who later passes a test to drive another type of vehicle (e.g. an LGV) will be subject to the special rules.

Where a person subject to the special rules accumulates six or more penalty points before the end of the two-year period (including any points acquired before passing the test) their licence will be revoked automatically. To regain the licence they must reapply for a provisional licence and may drive only as a learner until they pass a further driving test (also see Annexe 8 – Safety code for new drivers, pages 122–123.)
Law RT(ND)O

Note. This applies even if they pay for offences by fixed penalty. Drivers in the first group (UK, EU/EEA etc.) who already have a full licence for one type of vehicle are not affected by the special rules if they later pass a test to drive another type of vehicle.

Other consequences of offending
Where an offence is punishable by imprisonment, the vehicle used to commit the offence may be confiscated.
Law CJO Art 11

In addition to the penalties a court may decide to impose, the cost of insurance is likely to rise considerably following conviction for a serious driving offence. This is because insurance companies consider such drivers are more likely to be involved in a collision.

Drivers disqualified for alcohol related motoring offences twice within 10 years, or once if they are over two and a half times the legal limit, or those who refused to give a specimen, also have to satisfy the Driver and Vehicle Agency's Medical Branch that they do not have an alcohol problem and are otherwise fit to drive before a provisional licence is issued after the period of disqualification. Persistent misuse of drugs or alcohol may lead to the withdrawal of a driving licence.

6. Vehicle maintenance, safety and security

Vehicle maintenance

Take special care that lights, brakes, steering, exhaust system, seat belts, demisters, wipers and washers are all working. Also

- lights, indicators, reflectors, and number plates MUST be kept clean and clear
- windscreens and windows MUST be kept clean and free from obstructions to vision
- lights MUST be properly adjusted to prevent dazzling other road users. Extra attention needs to be paid to this if the vehicle is heavily loaded
- exhaust emissions MUST NOT exceed prescribed levels
- ensure your seat, seat belt, head restraint and mirrors are adjusted correctly before you drive
- ensure that items of luggage are securely stowed.

Laws RVLR 26 & 30 & CUR regs 35 & 74

Warning displays. Make sure that you understand the meaning of all warning displays on the vehicle instrument panel. Do not ignore warning signs, they could indicate a dangerous fault developing.

- When you turn the ignition key, warning lights will be illuminated but will go out when the engine starts (except the handbrake warning light). If they do not, or if they come on while you are driving, stop and investigate the problem, as there could be a serious fault.
- If the charge warning light comes on while you are driving, it may mean that the battery isn't charging. This should also be checked as soon as possible to avoid loss of power to lights and other electrical systems.

Window tints. You MUST NOT use a vehicle with excessively dark tinting fitted to the windscreen, or to the glass in any front window to either side of the driver. Window tinting applied during manufacture complies with the visual light transmittance (VLT) standards. There are no VLT limits for rear windscreens or rear passenger windows.

Laws RTO 1995 Art 58, CUR reg 37 & CUR(A)R 2005

Tyres. Tyres MUST be correctly inflated to the vehicle manufacturer's specification for the load being carried. Always refer to the vehicle's handbook or data. Tyres should also be free from certain cuts and other defects.

Cars, light vans and light trailers MUST have a tread depth of at least 1.6mm across the central three-quarters of the breadth of the tread and around the entire circumference.

Motorcycles, large vehicles and passenger-carrying vehicles MUST have a tread depth of at least 1mm across three-quarters of the breadth of the tread and in a continuous band around the entire circumference.

Mopeds should have visible tread.

Be aware that some vehicle defects can attract penalty points.

Law CUR reg 32

If a tyre bursts while you are driving, try to keep control of your vehicle. Grip the steering wheel firmly and allow the vehicle to roll to a stop at the side of the road.

If you have a flat tyre, stop as soon as it is safe to do so. Only change the tyre if you can do so without putting yourself or others at risk – otherwise call a breakdown service.

Tyre pressures. Check weekly. Do this before your journey, when tyres are cold. Warm or hot tyres may give a misleading reading. Your brakes and steering will be adversely affected by under-inflated or over-inflated tyres. Excessive or uneven tyre wear may be caused by faults in the braking or suspension systems, or wheels which are out of alignment. Have these faults corrected as soon as possible.

Spacesaver tyres, often referred to as 'get you home tyres', are speed or distance rated. Advice on their use can be found on the tyre or in the vehicle handbook.

Run flat tyres, which should only be used in conjunction with a tyre pressure monitoring system, enable vehicles to continue at reduced speeds for a limited distance following a puncture. Advice on their use can be found in the vehicle handbook.

Fluid levels. Check the fluid levels in your vehicle at least weekly. Low brake fluid may result in brake failure and a collision. Make sure you recognise the low fluid warning lights if your vehicle has them fitted.

Before winter. Ensure that the battery is well maintained and that there are appropriate anti-freeze agents in your radiator and windscreen bottle.

Other problems. If your vehicle
- pulls to one side when braking, it is most likely to be a brake fault or incorrectly inflated tyres. Consult a garage or mechanic immediately
- continues to bounce after pushing down on the front or rear, its shock absorbers are worn. Worn shock absorbers can seriously affect the operation of a vehicle and should be replaced
- smells of anything unusual such as burning rubber, petrol or an electrical fault; investigate immediately. Do not risk a fire.

Overheated engines or fire. Most engines are water-cooled. If your engine overheats you should wait until it has cooled naturally. Only then remove the coolant filler cap and add water or other coolant. If your vehicle catches fire, get the occupants out of the vehicle quickly and to a safe place. Do not attempt to extinguish a fire in the engine compartment, as opening the bonnet will make the fire flare. Call the Fire and Rescue Service.

Petrol stations/fuel tank/fuel leaks. Ensure that, when filling up your vehicle's tank or any fuel cans you are carrying, you do not spill fuel on the forecourt. Any spilled fuel should be immediately reported to the petrol station attendant. Diesel spillage is dangerous to other road users, particularly motorcyclists, as it will significantly reduce the level of grip between the tyres and road surface. Double-check for fuel leaks and make sure that
- you do not overfill your fuel tank
- the fuel cap is fastened securely
- the seal in the cap is not torn, perished or missing
- there is no visual damage to the cap or the fuel tank

Emergency fuel caps, if fitted, should form a good seal.
Never smoke, or use a mobile phone, on the forecourt of petrol stations as these are major fire risks and could cause an explosion.

Vehicle security

When you leave your vehicle you should
- remove the ignition key and engage the steering lock
- lock the car, even if you only leave it for a few minutes
- close the windows completely
- never leave children or pets in an unventilated car
- take all contents with you, or lock them in the boot. Remember, a potential thief might assume a carrier bag contains valuables
- never leave vehicle documents in the car.

For extra security fit an anti-theft device such as an alarm or immobiliser. When buying a new car check the level of built-in security features. Consider having your registration number etched on your car windows. This is a cheap and effective deterrent to professional thieves.

7. First aid on the road

In the event of an incident or collision, you can do a number of things to help, even if you have had no training.

1. Deal with danger

Further collisions and fire are the main dangers following a crash. Approach any vehicle involved with care. Switch off all engines and, if possible, warn other traffic. Stop anyone from smoking.

2. Get help

Try to get the assistance of bystanders. Get someone to call the appropriate emergency services as soon as possible. They will need to know the exact location of the incident and the number of vehicles involved.

3. Help those involved

DO NOT move casualties still in vehicles unless further danger is threatened. **DO NOT** remove a motorcyclist's helmet unless it is essential. Remember the casualty may be suffering from shock. **DO NOT** give them anything to eat or drink. **DO** try to make them warm and as comfortable as you can, but avoid unnecessary movement. **DO** give reassurance confidently and try not to leave them alone or let them wander into the path of other traffic.

4. Provide emergency care

Remember the letters **D R A B C:**
D – Danger – check that you are not in danger.
R – Response – try to get a response by asking questions and gently shaking their shoulders.
A – Airway – the airway should be clear and kept open. Place one hand on the forehead, two fingers under the chin and gently tilt the head back.
B – Breathing – normal breathing should be established. Once the airway is open, check breathing for up to 10 seconds.
C – Compressions – if they are not breathing normally, compressions should be administered to maintain circulation; place two hands in the centre of the chest and press down 4–5cms at a rate of 100/minute. You may only need one hand for a child. Give 30 chest compressions. Then tilt the head back gently, pinch the casualty's nostrils together and place your mouth over theirs. Give two breaths, each lasting one second (use gentle breaths for a small child).

If the casualty is unconscious and breathing, place them in the recovery position until medical help arrives

Bleeding. First check for anything that may be in the wound, such as glass. If there is nothing embedded apply firm pressure over the wound. Take care not to press on the object – build up padding on either side of it. Fasten a pad to the wound with a bandage or length of cloth. Use the cleanest material available. If a limb is bleeding, but not broken, raise it above the level of the heart to reduce the flow of blood. Any restriction of blood circulation for more than a short time could cause long-term injuries.

Burns. Try to cool the burn by dousing it with clean, cold water or similar non-toxic liquid for at least 10 minutes. Do not try to remove anything sticking to the burn.

5. Be prepared
Always carry a first aid kit. You could save a life by learning emergency aid and first aid from a qualified organisation, such as the local ambulance services, the St John Ambulance Association and Brigade, the Order of Malta Ambulance Corps, the British Red Cross or any suitable qualified body (see Useful websites, page 124 for contact details).

8. Safety code for new drivers
Once you have passed the driving test you will be able to drive on your own. This will provide you with lots of opportunities but you need to remain safe. Even though you have shown you have the skills you need to drive safely, many newly qualified drivers lack experience. You need to continue to develop your skills, especially anticipating other

road users' behaviour to avoid having a collision. As many as one new driver in five has some kind of collision in their first year of driving. This code provides advice to help you get through the first 12 months after passing the driving test, when you are most vulnerable, as safely as possible.

- Many of the worst collisions happen at night. Between midnight and 6am is a time of high risk for new drivers. Avoid driving then unless it's really necessary.
- If you are driving with passengers, you are responsible for their safety. Don't let them distract you or encourage you to take risks. Tell your passengers that you need to concentrate if you are to get to your destination safely.
- Never show off or try to compete with other drivers, particularly if they are driving badly.
- Don't drive if you have consumed any alcohol or taken drugs. Even over-the-counter medicines can affect your ability to drive safely – read the label to see if they may affect your driving.
- Make sure everyone in the car is wearing a seat belt throughout the journey.
- Keep your speed down – many serious collisions happen because the driver loses control, particularly on bends.
- Most new drivers have no experience of driving high-powered or sporty cars. Unless you have learnt to drive in such a vehicle you need to get plenty of experience driving on your own before driving a more powerful car.
- Driving while uninsured is an offence. See Annexe 3 for information on types of insurance cover.

REMEMBER that under the New Drivers Order you will have your licence revoked if you get six penalty points on your licence within two years of passing your first driving test. You will need to pass both the theory and practical tests again to get back your full licence.

You could consider taking further training or obtaining an advanced driving qualification which could save you money on your insurance as well as helping you reduce your risk of being involved in a collision. There are three ways to find out more:
- internet – www.roadsafetyni.gov.uk
- telephone – DOE Road Safety Branch 028 9054 0040
- Email – roadsafety@doeni.gov.uk

Other information

Metric conversions

The conversions given throughout *The Highway Code* are rounded but a detailed conversion chart is shown below.

Miles	Kilometres	Miles	Kilometres
1.00	1.61	40.00	64.37
5.00	8.05	45.00	72.42
10.00	16.09	50.00	80.47
15.00	24.14	55.00	88.51
20.00	32.19	60.00	96.56
25.00	40.23	65.00	104.60
30.00	48.28	70.00	112.65
35.00	56.33		

Useful websites

www.sja.org.uk St John Ambulance Association and Brigade
www.orderofmalta.ie Order of Malta Ambulance Corps
www.redcross.co.uk British Red Cross
www.roadsafetyni.gov.uk
www.roadsni.gov.uk
www.trafficwatchni.com
www.psni.police.uk
www.dvani.gov.uk
www.roadsafetycouncil.com
www.dft.gov.uk
www.rsa.ie
www.nra.ie

Further reading

Best practice

Further information about good driving and riding practice can be found in The Driving Standards Agency books *The Official DSA Guide to Driving – the essential skills* and *The Official DSA Guide to Riding – the essential skills*. Information specifically for drivers of large vehicles can be found in *The Official DSA Guide to Driving Goods Vehicles* and *The Official DSA Guide to Driving Buses and Coaches*.

The Blue Badge Scheme

Information on this scheme can be found on the Department for Regional Development Roads Service website www.roadsni.gov.uk

Code of Practice for Horse-Drawn Vehicles

The Code of Practice is available from the Department for Transport, Transport Technology and Standards Division 6, 2nd Floor, Great Minster House, 76 Marsham Street, London SW1P 4DR.
Tel: 0207 944 2078

Roadworks

A leaflet giving further information on driving through roadworks can be obtained from Highways Agency Publications, tel: 0870 1226 236, quoting reference number HA113/04. For general Highways Agency information, tel: 08457 504030 or email info@highways.gsi.gov.uk

Appendix

Roundabouts are safe and simple if you know and use these rules

Many drivers are satisfied with their own use of roundabouts, but believe others do it all wrong! Before criticising other drivers' roundabout behaviour, check your knowledge of the rules.

Why roundabouts?

When used properly, roundabouts can smooth traffic flow at busy junctions. Vehicles can enter and leave roundabouts by different roads with less inconvenience or danger. They are really circular, clockwise one-way traffic systems enabling several traffic streams to mix.

The rules for using roundabouts

Give way: the most important rule – when entering a roundabout, give way to traffic on the roundabout, unless road markings or signs say otherwise. If the way is clear keep moving. Stopping at a clear roundabout slows traffic and can cause frustrating delays.

A roundabout entrance is usually marked by a single broken line across the road. Sometimes you may find other markings. At some roundabouts one traffic lane might be allowed to flow free; there will be road markings or signs to show this.

Speed: approach so that you can stop and give way if necessary. Approaching too fast could make other drivers on the roundabout think that you are going to drive in front of them. They could brake or swerve and perhaps cause a collision. If you approach too fast and brake hard at a roundabout entrance you could also cause a collision by panicking a following driver who might skid into the back of your vehicle.

On the roundabout, you should drive according to road, weather and traffic conditions as well as the road-holding qualities of your vehicle.

Position and signals: being correctly positioned and signalling clearly in good time helps other road users. Knowing and following the rules improves traffic flow and safety at roundabouts.

While this appendix provides general advice, other factors such as signs, road markings and the position and type of other vehicles can influence the choice of lane. Where there are signs or road markings which indicate appropriate lanes, these should assume priority over the following procedures.

Correct roundabout procedure

Imagine that you are approaching a busy roundabout with six converging roads. Follow the advice in the diagrams. Treat the roundabout as if it were a clock face. All movement on roundabouts is clockwise.

Always assume that your approach is from the six o'clock position. Approach at the correct speed and in the right gear. Always signal your intentions clearly. If there is no traffic at or on the roundabout you may take the shortest and most convenient route through it. Cancel your signal after leaving the roundabout.

Now that you know the rules, show a good example to other drivers by following them every time. They may even copy your driving style and do it right too!

1. Taking the first exit (b) at 8 o'clock

Approach Left lane
Signal All-round observation and left-turn indicator on approach
On roundabout Keep in left lane
Exit Check mirrors before leaving roundabout and keep left-turn indicator going until just after leaving roundabout

2. Taking the second exit (c) at 10 o'clock

Approach Left lane
Signal All-round observation; no approach signal
On roundabout Keep in left lane
Exit Check mirrors and indicate left when you have passed exit (b) before the one you want to take (c)

3. Taking the third exit (d) at 12 o'clock

Approach Left lane
Signal No approach signal
On roundabout Keep in left lane (use right lane if approach was in right lane)
Exit Check mirrors and indicate left when you have passed exit (c) before the one you want to take (d)

4. Taking the fourth exit (e) at 2 o'clock

Approach Right lane
Signal All-round observation and indicate right on approach
On roundabout Keep in right lane near centre of roundabout; keep right-turn indicator going
Exit Check mirrors and change to left-turn indicator when you have passed exit (d) before the one you want to take (e). Check mirrors, glance over left shoulder and ease into left lane for exit (e)

5. Taking the fifth exit (f) at 4 o'clock

Approach Right lane
Signal All-round observation and indicate right on approach
On roundabout Keep in right lane near centre of roundabout; keep right-turn indicator going
Exit Check mirrors and change to left-turn indicator when you have passed exit (e) before the one you want to take (f). Check mirrors, glance over left shoulder and ease into left lane for exit (f)

The Highway Code

Index

References are to rule numbers, except those numbers in **bold italics**, which refer to page numbers

ABS *see* Braking/brakes
Active Traffic Management
  (ATM) Signs   269
Advanced stop lines   61, 71, 178
Airbags   101
Alcohol   68, 95, **115–116**
Animals   47–58, 214–215, 286
  horses   47–56, 163, 187, 214–215, 286
    level crossings   294
    motorways   253, 275
Arm signals   53, 55, 67, 74, 103, **93–95**
Attitude   147

B
Baby seats see Rear–facing baby seats
Battery   **118**
Bell   **108**
Bends   2, 125, 146, 160, 166, 231, 243
Blind spots   159, 161, 202, 267
Blue Badge scheme   45, **125**
Box junctions   174, **106**
Brake warning lights   103, 235, **93**
Braking/brakes   117–122, 231, 237, **118**
  ABS braking   120
  condition of   **118**
Breakdowns   274
  level crossings   299
  motorways   274–277
Bright sunlight *see* Dazzle
Bus lanes   141, 240
  crossing   12, 183
  cyclists   65
  one-way streets   11, 143
  overtaking   165
  parking   240
  turning   183
Bus stops   243
  give way   223
  overtaking   167
  pedestrians   206, 223, 243
  school   209
Buses   223, 265
  board/alight   32
  overtaking   65, 167
  school   209

C
Car phones *see* Mobile phones
Caravans   98, 160, 250, 265
Central islands   7, 20, 28, 30, 197, 243
Changing lanes   133,134, 151
Chicanes   153
Child locks   102
Child restraints   99–100, 102
Children
  cars   99–100, 102, **121**
  Green Cross Code   7, 30
  horses   215
  on motorways   275
  other goods vehicles   99–100, 102
  parking   239
  pedestrian crossings   18, 29
  pedestrians   7, 202, 204–210, 304
  vans   99–100, 102
  young   4
Clearways   240, **97**
Climbing/crawler lane   139
Clothing
  cyclists   59
  drivers   97, 228
  horse riders   49
  motorcyclists   83–84, 86–87
  pedestrians   3, 5, 17, 58
Coasting   122
Concentration   148–150, 288
Consideration   144, 147
Conspicuity
  cyclists   59–60
  horse riders   49–51
  horse-drawn vehicles   48
  motorcyclists   86–87
  pedestrians   3, 5, 17, 58
Contraflow systems   290
Controlled crossings 7, 22–30, 79–82,   196–199
Controlled parking zones   238, 245
Controls   97
Country roads   154
Courtesy   147
Crossing the road   7–35
  cyclists   79–82
Crossings *see* Pedestrian crossings
Crossroads (unmarked)   146

Crosswinds 232
Cruise control 150
Cycle lanes and tracks
  cyclists 61–63, 65
  dogs 56
  drivers 140
  horse riders 54
  parking 140, 240
  pedestrians 11–13, 62, 66
  turning 183
Cycle maintenance/choice **108**
Cycle-only crossing 81
Cyclists and cycling 59–82, 211–213, 253
  junctions 72–75,170, 177–178,
    180, 182–183, 211
  overtaking/clearance 65, 129, 160,
    163, 212, 232
  pedestrians 13, 62, 66
  rear observation 67, 212
  roundabouts 76–78, 187
  routes 61–63, 65
  traffic lights 69, 71, 79–82, 177–178
  trams 306
  turning 74, 212

D
Dangerous goods 284–285
Dazzle 93, 115, 236–237
Decriminalised Parking **78**
Demisters 229, 235, **118**
Diagonal stripes/chevrons 130, **104**
Direction indicators *see* Signals
Disabled 204, 207
  cyclists 62
  drivers on motorway 253, 278
  pedestrian crossings 26
  vehicles for 36–46, 220, 239, 241, 250
Distractions 148–150
Documents 286–287, **110–112**
Dogs (including guide dogs) 56–57, 207
Double white lines 128–129, 165, 240,
    104
Drinking and driving 68, 95, **115–118**
Driver and Vehicle Agency
  Enforcement Officer
  signals and livery **95**
  stopping powers 107
Driving, general advice 144–156
Driving licence **108–113**
Drugs/medicine 68, 96

Dual carriageways
  crossing/turning 137, 173
  cyclists 75
  three-lane 138
  two-lane 137
Dull weather 115

E
Electric vehicles 224
Emergency telephones 275, 280, 283
Emergency vehicles 31, 219, 281
Environmental issues 123
Equestrian Crossings 27, 79, 199
Exhaust systems **118**
Eyesight/vision 92–94

F
Fatigue 91, 237, 262
Filter lights 177
Fire **120**
First aid 283, **121–122**
Fitness to drive 90–91
Flashing amber beacons 220, 225
Flashing headlights 60, 110–111
Flashing signals
  emergency 31, 219, 281
  headlights 110, 111
  level crossings 293
  motorways 257–258, 270
  police 31, 106, 219, 281
  school 208
  slow-moving vehicles 220, 225
  tramways 33
Fluorescent/reflective clothing
  breakdowns 274
  cyclists 59
  horse riders 50
  motorcyclists 86–87
  pedestrians 3, 5, 17
Fog 234–236
  lights 114, 226, 236
  motorways 235, 255, 260
  parking 251
Footpaths
  cyclists 13, 62, 64, 70
  drivers 145
  horses 54
  pedestrians 1–2, 4, 13
  prohibited vehicles 157–158
Footway *see* Pavement

The Highway Code

G
Give way
  junctions   172, 183, 185, 189, 206
  motorways   259
Gopeds *see* Prohibited vehicles
Green Cross Code   7, 30

H
Hard shoulder *see* Motorways
Hazard warning lights 116, 274, 277–278, 283
Hazard warning plates   284, *107*
Head restraints   97, *118*
Headlamps and headlights 113–115, 226, 235,
                                  239
  motorcycle   87
Headlight flashing   110–111
Helmets
  cyclists   59
  horse riders   49
  incidents   283, *121*
  motorcyclists   83, 86, 283, *121*
High-Occupancy Vehicle
  Lanes (HOVs)   142, *102*
Highways Agency Traffic Officers (HATO)
  stopping powers   108
Hills
  control   160
  parking   243, 252
Home zones   206, 218
Horn   112, 214
Horse-drawn vehicles   47–48, 215, *125*
Horse riders   49–55, 163,
                 187, 214, 215, 253
Hot weather   237
HOVs *see* High-Occupancy Vehicle Lanes

I
Ice cream vans   206
Icy weather   126, 195, 213, 228–231, 260
In-vehicle technology   149–150
Incident support vehicles   219
Incidents   281–287, *121–123*
  dangerous goods   284–285
  documentation   286–287
  first aid   283, *121–122*
  flashing lights   281
  level crossing   299
  motorway   283
  warning signs   281
Inexperienced drivers 204, 217, *122–123*

Insurance   287, *110–112*
Islands   7, 20, 28, 30, 197, 243

J
Junctions *see* Road junctions

L
L plates   *108–109, 112*
Lamps and lights
  conditions/maintenance 113, 229, *108, 118*
  cyclists   60
  horses   51
  pedestrians   5, 58
  vehicles   113–116, 249–251, 274
  see also Headlamps and headlights
Lane discipline   133–143, 288
  dual carriageways   137–138
  motorways   263–265
  multi-lane carriageways   133–139
  one-way streets   143
  roundabouts   184–187
  single carriageways   135
Lane dividers   131, *104*
Large vehicles   126, 160, 164,
               221–222, 233, 294
  see also Long/large vehicles
Lay-bys   249–250
Learner drivers   204, 217, 253, *110–112*
Level crossings 34, 54, 82, 167, 243, 291–299
Lighting requirements   5, 43, 48, 60,
           113–115, 226, 229, 235–236
Lights *see* Headlamps and headlights,
  Lamps and lights
Lines and lanes   127–132, 136–143,
                   184–185, *104*
  see also Traffic signs/road markings
Littering from vehicles   147
Loading and unloading   246–247
Loads   98, 250
Long/large vehicles *see also* Large vehicles
  cyclists   73, 78
  junctions   170, 173
  roadworks   288
  roundabouts   78, 187–188
  trams   300–307

M
Maintenance of vehicles   *118–120*
Manoeuvring 159–190, 200–203
  large vehicles   221

motorcycles	88
Medicines	68, 96
Merging in turn	134, 288
Metric conversion table	**124**
Miniature motorcycles (mini-motos)	
see Prohibited vehicles	
Mini-roundabouts	188–190
Mirrors	97, 161, 184, 202, 229, 288–289, **118**
changing lanes	133
fog	234–235
motorways	254, 267
moving off	97, 159
overtaking	163, 267
turning	179–180, 182
Mobile phones	97,149, 270, 275, 278, 283, 285, **120**
MOT	**111**
Motorcycle licence	**108–109**
Motorcyclists	83–98, 160, 211–213, 232–233, 250, 253, 306
conspicuity	86–87
junctions	88, 170, 180, 182, 211–213
learners	204, 217, 253, **108–110**
night riding	87
overall stopping distance	126, 227, 230, 235, 260
overtaking	88, 163, 230
rear observation	88, 212
roundabouts	187
turning	88
winter	230, **119**
Motor tricycles see Prohibited vehicles	
Motorways	253–273
breakdowns	274–278
contraflow systems	290
emergency telephones	275, 283
fog	234
hard shoulder	275, 290
obstructions	279–280
pedestrians	6
road works	288
signals/signs/flashing lights	255–258, 281
stopping and parking	91, 240
studs	132
Moving off	159

N

Narrow/winding roads see Country roads	
Navigation systems	150

New drivers	**117, 122–123**
Night	
animals	51, 58
cyclists	60
driving	94
lights see Lamps and lights	
motorways	267
overtaking	163
parking	248–251
pedestrians	3, 5, 17
speed	125

O

Obstructions	279–280
cyclists	67, 70
lines/lanes	288–289
motorways	280
vehicles	146, 163, 242
Older drivers	216
Older pedestrians	62, 204, 207
One-way streets	143
crossing	11
horses	53
Organised walks	5
Other stopping procedures	107–108
Overhead electric lines	292, 307
Overtaking	135, 160, 162–169, 230
animals	163, 214–215
before overtaking	162
bus lanes	165
being overtaken	168–169
crossings	165, 191
cyclists	65, 67, 129, 160, 163, 211–212, 232
dual carriageways	137–138
horse riders	215
long vehicles	160, 164, 169
motorcyclists	88, 163, 211–212, 230
motorways	267–268
queues	163, 288
single-track roads	155
trams	167, 301, 303

P

Parked vehicles	
Green Cross Code	7
pedestrians	7, 14, 193, 206
Parking	238–252, 302
bicycles	70
fog	251

goods vehicles	246–247	Powered wheelchairs and	
hazard warning lights	116	powered mobility scooters	36–46, 220, 253
level crossings	291	Prohibited vehicles	157–158
motorways	91, 240	Protective clothing	48, 50, 59, 83
at night	248–250	Puffin crossings	23–24, 28, 191–194, 199, 240
pedestrian crossings	191	pedestrians	7, 18, 23–24
single-track roads	156	cyclists	79
Passengers, carriage of	99, 275		
by cyclists	68	**Q**	
by learners	***109***	Quad bikes *see* Prohibited vehicles	
by horse riders	53	Queues	169
by motorcyclists	85, ***109***	long vehicles	169
Passing places	155–156	overtaking	163, 288
Pavements		pedestrian crossings	192–193
cycling	64, 70	Quiet lanes	206, 218
driving	145		
horses	54	**R**	
parking	244	Railway level crossings	34, 167, 243, 291–294
pedestrians	1–2, 4	tactile surfaces	34
prohibited vehicles	157–158	Rear-facing baby seats	101
repairs	35	Rear fog lamps	114, 226, 236
Pedestrian crossings	18–30, 191–199, 240	Rear view mirrors	
		condition	229
controlled	7, 21–28, 80, 196–199	driving	161, 184, 202
level	34	in fog	234–235
equestrian	27, 79, 199	Red routes	240, 247, ***105***
pelican	7, 22, 23, 24, 79, 196–198	Reflective clothing	
puffin	7, 23–24, 79, 199	cyclists	59
staggered	28	horse riders	50
toucan	7, 25–26, 80, 199	motorcyclists	87
traffic lights	21	pedestrians	3, 5, 17, 58
zebra	7, 19–20, 79, 195	powered mobility vehicles	43
Pedestrians	1–35, 125, 146, 152, 154, 202, 204–210, 223, 244	Reflective studs *see* Road studs	
		Reflectors	48, 60, ***108, 118***
blind/deaf/older	26, 62, 66, 204, 207, 244	Residential area	
cyclists	13, 62, 66	lights	115
junctions	8, 170, 180, 206	pedestrians	152, 206
motorways	6, 253, 271	speed	152
safety	1, 204–210, 239	Restricted drivers	***112***
safety barriers	9	Reversing	200–203, 206, 263
tramways	33, 206, 223, 304	Riding	
Pelican crossings	22, 28, 191–194, 196–198, 240	cycles	61–82
		horses	52–55
cyclists	79	motorcycles	83–88
pedestrians	7, 18, 22, 24, 28	Road humps	153
Penalties	***115–118, 123***	Road junctions	88, 146, 167, 170–183, 211
Pillion passengers	83, 85, ***109***	cyclists	72–75, 170, 177–180, 182–183
Police stopping procedures	106	lanes	177
Positioning at junctions	175–179, 186, 235	parking	243
on the road	160	pedestrians	8, 170, 180, 206

Road signs *see* Traffic signs
Road studs   132
Road traffic law   **113–118**
Road users requiring extra care   204–218
Roadworks   35, 132, 167, 288–290
  contraflow systems   290
  motorways   289
Roundabouts   184–190
  cyclists   76–78, 187
  horse riders   55, 187
  long vehicles   78, 187–188
  mini-roundabouts   186,188–189
  multiple roundabouts   190
  road markings   184–185
  specific advice   **126–129**
Route guidance and navigation systems   150

S

Safety barriers, pedestrian   9
Safety helmets
  cyclists   59
  horse riders   49
  motorcyclists   83, 86, 283, **121**
School crossing patrols   7, 29, 105, 208, 210
  overtaking   167, 209
  pole positions   **95**
Seat belts   99–100, 102, **118**
Security of vehicles   239, **120**
Separation distance
  cyclists   160, 163, 212
  fog   235
  large vehicles   222
  motorways   260
  overall stopping distance   126, 151, 227,
                             230, 235, 260, 289
  overtaking   163–164, 222
Shared cycle routes   13, 62
Signals   103–112
  arm   53, 55, 67, 74, 103, 93–95
  buses   223
  cyclists   67, 74
  flashing   31,110–111, 281, 293
  horse riders   53, 55, 215
  junctions   103, 179, 182, 186
  lane changes   133
  large goods vehicles   187
  motorcyclists   88, 93
  motorways   255–258, 266, 269–270
  moving off   159
  other road users   103–104

overtaking   163, 267
pedestrian crossings   22–27,196, 198–199
police/wardens/schools/other 105–108, **94–95**
Single carriageways   135–136
Single-track roads   155–156
Skidding   119
  ABS braking   120
  avoiding   231
Slip roads   259, 270, 272–273
Slippery roads *see* Wet roads
Slow-moving traffic   151, 163, 288
Slow-moving vehicles   169, 220, 224–225,
                             253, 264, 288
  climbing/crawler lanes   139
  flashing amber beacons   225
  level crossings   294
  queues   169
Smoking   148
Snow   228–231
Soft tarmac   237
Speed limits 124–125, 146, 152, 257, 261, 288
Speed limiters   222, 265
Steering condition   **118–119**
  winter driving   231
Stopping/parking   238–252
  bus lanes   240
  cycle lanes   140
  level crossings   291, 294
  mobile phones   149
  motorways   91, 240, 270–271
  on pavements   244, 246
  outside schools   238
  passing places   155–156
  pedestrian crossings 191–192, 196–197, 240
  single-track roads   155–156
Stopping distance   126, 151, 227, 230,
                             235, 260, 289
  see also Separation distance
Street/pavement repairs   35

T

Tactile paving   10
  surfaces at level crossings   34
Telephones
  mobile phones   149, 278, 283, 285, **120**
  railway   294, 297, 299
  motorways   275, 283
Theory test   **108–109**
Tinted glasses   94
Tinting, windows   **118**

The Highway Code

Tiredness/illness 90–91, 237, 262
Toucan crossings 7, 18, 25, 199, 240
  cyclists 61, 80
  pedestrians 7, 25, 80
Towing 98, 160
Traffic calming 153
Traffic lights 109, 184–185, **92**
  cyclists 69, 71, 80–82, 177–178
  green filter lights 177
  junctions 175–178
  level crossings 293, 296
  pedestrians 21
  trams 300–301
Traffic officers
  stopping procedures 107–108
  signals and livery **95**
Traffic signs/road markings 109,127–131,
    134, 142, 143, 184–185,
    234, 238, 288, 298, **96–106**
  see also Lines & lanes
  cyclists 63, 69, 71, 140, 178
  junctions 171–172, 174–176, 178, 181, 184
  traffic lights 109, 175–178, **92**
Trailers 98, 160, 246, 265
Tramways 33, 223, 300–307
  cyclists 82
  overtaking 167, 301
  parking 240, 243, 302
  pedestrians 33, 206, 223, 303
  turning left 183
Transporting animals 98
Triangles 172, 274
Tunnels 126
Turning left
  bus/tram/cycle lanes 183
  junctions 182–183
  one-way streets 143
  roundabouts 186
Turning right
  box junctions 174
  cyclists 74, 212
  dual carriageways 137, 173
  diagonal stripes/chevrons 130
  junctions 179–181
  one-way streets 143
  roundabouts 186
  traffic lights 176–177
Two-second rule 126
  see also Separation distance
Tyres 227, **108, 119**

U
U-turn 188

V
Vehicle condition 89, 97 **118–120**
Vehicle Excise Duty **111**
Vehicle licence **108–110**
Vehicle markings 284–285, **107**
Vehicle Registration Certificate **111**
Vehicle security 239, **120**
Vehicle Test Certificate (MOT) **110**
Visibility/view 94, 159–160, 162–164,
    229, 274
  fog 226, 236
  junctions 88, 170, 211
  lights 114–115, 226, 236
  motorways 235, 267
  overtaking 162–163, 166, 267
  pedestrians/cyclists 3, 7, 146, 160, 170
  reversing 202, 206
  snow 228–229
Vision 92
Vulnerable pedestrians 207

W
Waiting 238
Warning lights **118**
Water (on brakes) 121
Wet/icy/slippery roads 213, 227–231, 237, 306
  pedestrian crossings 195
  speed limits 125
  stopping distances 126, 227, 230, 260
White lines 127–132, **104**
Windscreens/washers/wipers 229, 235, **118**
Windy weather 232–233
Winter driving **119**
  see also Snow, Wet/icy/slippery roads

Y
Yellow lines 238, 247, **105–106**
Young children 4, 7

Z
Zebra crossings 191–195, 240
  pedestrians 7, 18–20
  cyclists 79
  with a central island 20